Total School Cluster Grouping & Differentiation

A Comprehensive, Research-based Plan for Raising Student Achievement & Improving Teacher Practices

**Marcia Gentry &
Rebecca L. Mann**

EDITOR:

RACHEL A. KNOX

CREATIVE LEARNING PRESS, INC., PO BOX 320, MANSFIELD CENTER, CT, 06250
888-518-8004 • WWW.CREATIVELEARNINGPRESS.COM

ACKNOWLEDGEMENTS

I would like to acknowledge and thank my graduate school mentors, Sally M. Reis, Joseph S. Renzulli, Robert K. Gable, Steven V. Owen, Karen Westberg, and E. Jean Gubbins, whose guidance, teaching, and support made the work on this model possible. I am fortunate and proud to have studied with each of you and to follow in your footsteps. Sally, your encouragement resulted in this work—thank-you. I credit Bessie Duncan, whose work with cluster grouping in the Detroit Public Schools laid the foundation for the development of this model. I am grateful for the support of my husband, William Byers, and my parents, Roger and Jacky Gentry. I dedicate this book to my daughter, Gentry Lee, whose journey though school provides me daily with a fresh perspective on our educational system. This work is for her and other students who, like her, deserve the best education that we can provide them.

—Marcia Gentry

I would like to thank Eric, my husband, for his never-ending patience and support. I am also grateful for the enthusiastic encouragement and gentle nudges I received from my mom, Margaret Collins. I dedicate this book to my children, Matthew and Sara, who inspired me to pursue a career in education, and to my students, who continue to amaze and motivate me. Finally, I would like to acknowledge the dedicated teachers with whom I have worked who eagerly embraced student-focused differentiation; our shared journey has been inspiring.

—Rebecca Mann

We both deeply appreciate Purdue graduate students Jillian Gates, Jamie MacDougall, and Michelle Strutz whose editorial comments strengthened this work. We thank Rachel Knox, editor at Creative Learning Press, for her valuable edits and suggestions.

TABLE OF CONTENTS

LIST OF FIGURES

LIST OF TABLES

FOREWORD

I am delighted that this important, practical, easy-to-read manual is available. It provides new information for teachers and administrators who are interested in using cluster grouping as a service for gifted and high potential students as well as a method for more effectively and efficiently meeting the needs of all students. As you become familiar with the kind of cluster grouping Drs. Gentry and Mann detail here—that is, *total school cluster grouping*—you may find it hard not to rush to implement. However, as the authors point out, grouping alone has a little, if any, effect on academic gain and other outcomes. In order for total school cluster grouping to benefit students, educators must go a step further and make the most of what grouping offers: classrooms with small groups of students clustered so that they reflect a limited range in abilities (rather than the complete range of abilities from low to high found in most classrooms). Instead of all teachers trying to teach all things appropriately to all students wherever their abilities, talents, and interests may lie, Total School Cluster Grouping allows educators to focus on a small range of abilities and differentiate the curriculum, materials, process, and products specifically to meet those students' needs and characteristics. Marcia Gentry's research on cluster grouping has proven that this practice raises achievement and promotes talent development in all students. When grouped appropriately and given differentiated instruction, students develop more responsibility in academic planning and in completing work and achieve gains in achievement levels.

The suggestions discussed in this book are based on sound educational research with related research-based classroom practices that will result in positive academic gains. It is a much-needed book in today's pressured environment. I hope that all educators who are interested in having their students become more engaged in their own learning, raise their achievement, and enjoy school more read this important new book.

Sally Reis, Ph. D.
University of Connecticut

INTRODUCTION

Our work with what has become the Total School Cluster Grouping Model began in earnest in the late 1980s with the implementation, development, and refinement of the model. We studied the model in the 1990s and found that all students where the model was implemented benefited from the model by achieving at higher levels and by having their teachers recognize them as higher achieving. We also found that classroom teachers implemented strategies and curriculum typically reserved for gifted programs. Since then, we have helped many school districts across the country implement this model. Our original research has served as a foundation for larger-scale research and program implementation currently underway by other researchers. We have received clinical and anecdotal reports of achievement, identification, and teacher practice results similar to the results we found and reported. Due to the continued popularity and increased implementation across the country, we have initiated a new controlled study of this program. Currently, we are in the middle of this longitudinal study replicating the original work on this model and thus far have had strikingly similar results.

Total School Cluster Grouping offers educators a common-sense, whole-school approach to student placement, staff-development, and differentiation. This model uses talent-development approaches typically found in gifted education programs to improve the achievement and performance of all children in a school. As such, this model focuses on student abilities and how educators can enhance every student's strengths, skills, and confidence by using grouping and enriched instruction.

This book represents a culmination of our knowledge to date of the best way to implement this model in elementary schools with two or more classes per grade level. We devoted Part I to the specifics of the Total School Cluster Grouping Model. In Chapter 1 we define cluster grouping, examine the theory and research that underlies the model, define terms, and consider cluster grouping in the wider context of ability grouping. In Chapter 2 we define the Total School Cluster Grouping Model, describe how to flexibly identify the performance levels of all students in the school, and then discuss how to thoughtfully place them in classrooms in a manner that helps ensure that their educational needs will be met. We conclude this chapter with a discussion of data collection and evaluation, talking with parents, and general suggestions for successful implementation. In Chapter 3 we address professional development, classroom practices, the use of grouping, and the role of the teacher—all components for effective model implementation. We end Part I with an overview of a continuum of elementary education talent development services and a discussion of how this model fits with other educational programs and efforts.

In Part II we address differentiation in the cluster-grouped classroom, beginning with Chapter 5, which provides a definition and an overview of essential elements for differentiation. Chapter 6 deals with specific strategies, such as curriculum compacting and tiered assignments, that teachers can use to develop a differentiated learning environment in their cluster-grouped classrooms. In Chapter 7 we introduce inquiry-based instructional strategies such as questioning techniques that require high-levels of thought by students and teachers. We focus on open-ended activities and the use of individual and small-group investigations to stimulate learning that reaches beyond the basic standards. Finally in Chapter 8, we introduce the concept of student-focused differentiation, a brand of differentiation that is designed to increase student motivation and decrease teacher preparation by putting the student in charge of his or her learning.

Appendix A provides teachers with instruments, forms, and checklists to help them learn about their students' interests and learning preferences. It also contains other forms to help guide independent studies and provide students with challenge. Appendix B contains recommendations of quality resources that teachers can use to continue their quest toward effective differentiation in their classrooms. This list is not meant to be exhaustive, but rather a place to begin, in that it contains high quality materials, websites, and recommendations that we know work for teachers and their students.

We believe that Total School Cluster Grouping and effective curricular and instructional differentiation using principles of talent development can benefit all students and staff. Our research findings support this belief. This book offers educators a model for rethinking traditional approaches to classroom placement and grouping. This model can, quite simply, help teachers more effectively meet the educational needs of all students.

PART I

1

WHAT IS CLUSTER GROUPING?

AN INTRODUCTION TO TOTAL SCHOOL CLUSTER GROUPING

Total School Cluster Grouping is a specific form of cluster grouping that has a research base, theoretical rationale, and model for successful implementation in schools. This book focuses on why an elementary school staff would want to consider developing a Total School Cluster Grouping program, followed by how to implement this model successfully in schools, and effective strategies for differentiating in the cluster-grouped classroom. Total School Cluster Grouping aims to

* provide full-time services to high-achieving, high-ability elementary students,
* help all students improve their academic achievement and educational self-efficacy,
* help teachers more effectively and efficiently meet the diverse needs of their students,
* weave gifted education and talent development "know-how" into the fabric of all educational practices in the school.

Prior to examining the details of the Total School Cluster Grouping Model, we will consider the model in the context of general cluster grouping and other ability grouping practices to provide you with information concerning what Total School Cluster Grouping is and what it is not.

Cluster grouping is a widely recommended and often used strategy for meeting the needs of high-achieving and high-ability students in the regular elementary classroom. Its use has gained popularity in recent years because of the move toward inclusive education, budget cuts, and heterogeneous grouping policies that have eliminated programs for gifted students (Purcell, 1994; Renzulli, 2005; State of the States, 2007).

When viewed in the larger context of school reform and extending gifted education services to more students, cluster grouping can reach and benefit teachers and students beyond those in traditional gifted programs.

Cluster grouping is generally defined as placing a group of gifted, high-achieving, or high-ability students in an elementary classroom with other students. There are many experts in the field of gifted education who recommend this approach. They often suggest a specific number of high-ability children—say, six to eight—to comprise the cluster, and they specify that the rest of the class should be heterogeneous. Further, many applications of cluster grouping are often only concerned with the identified high-ability children and what occurs in their designated classroom. Composition of and practices within the other classrooms are frequently ignored, as the perceived purpose of cluster grouping is to serve the identified children.

However, because cluster grouping places the highest-achieving students in one classroom and affects the composition of all other classrooms, it affects all students and teachers in the school. Therefore, cluster grouping should not only be viewed as only a program for gifted students, but also as a total school program. Through staff development, flexible placement, and grouping integrated with the regular school structure, cluster grouping offers a means for improving curriculum, instruction, and student achievement throughout the school.

The benefits of a thoughtfully implemented cluster grouping program include:

* challenging high achievers by placing them together in one classroom, thus enabling new talents to emerge among students in other classrooms and allowing them opportunities to become academic leaders;
* increasing the ability of all teachers to meet the individual academic needs of their students by reducing the range of student achievement levels in all classrooms;
* improving how teachers view their students with respect to ability and achievement;
* improving student achievement among students from all achievement levels;
* increasing the number of students identified as high achieving and decreasing the number of students identified as low achieving;
* extending gifted education services to more students in a school than those students identified as "gifted and talented";
* bringing gifted education staff development, methods, and materials to all teachers in a school;

* providing full time placement and services for students identified as high achieving;

* providing a seamless fit with a continuum of gifted and talented services for students;

* helping teachers work together to plan effective differentiated curriculum and instruction for students at various levels of achievement and readiness;

* on-going student strength and ability assessment and identification;

* offering students the opportunity to grow and develop by receiving services that match their current levels of achievement in various subjects.

THEORETICAL UNDERPINNINGS

In educational settings across the country, meeting the needs of high-achieving students is a perpetual struggle. Staff, budget, and resource constraints frequently limit or exhaust the possibility of programming for the highest achievers. As gifted and talented programs are eliminated across the country due to the on-going struggle schools face to comply with No Child Left Behind and increased test-score account-ability, parents and educators face an increased challenge of providing appropriate educational services to high-ability students who find basic standards unchal-lenging. Cluster grouping has experienced an increase in popularity, due largely to research findings that showed improved achievement test scores of students across all achievement levels (Gentry & Owen, 1999). District personnel across the country are searching for a way to improve student performance on tests, and cluster grouping has the potential to help them achieve this goal.

Many variations in definitions and applications of cluster grouping have been noted but three non-negotiable components consistently prevail (Gentry, 1999). First, groups of students (varying in number from three to more than ten) identified as gifted, high-achieving, or high-ability are placed in classrooms with students of other achievement levels. Second, teachers differentiate curriculum and instruc-tion for the high-achieving students in the clustered classroom. Third, successful teachers of high-ability students have an interest or background in working with gifted students. These three components drive the success of cluster grouping and serve as the foundational touchstones for this book. In order to understand the phil-osophical and structural nuances of cluster grouping, one first needs to consider definitions, history, research, misconceptions, and theoretical underpinnings of such programming.

UNDERSTANDING CLUSTER GROUPING IN THE CONTEXT OF ABILITY GROUPING

Cluster grouping is an organizational model that should be discussed in the broader context of ability grouping. Thousands of studies on the positive and negative effects of full-time ability grouping exist. In the last decade-and-a-half, at least nine analyses of the effects of full-time grouping have been compiled (Rogers, 2002). Conflicting results, conclusions, and opinions exist regarding ability grouping. Ability grouping has been touted as both an effective means for promoting student achievement and an evil force contributing to the downfall of America's schools. However, the "real" answer lies somewhere in the middle and depends largely upon the context and application of the ability grouping. During this raging controversy, teachers are doing their best to meet students' individual needs within their classrooms. With the recent and emotional calls for full-scale elimina-tion of ability grouping, the advent of full inclusion, the addition of few resources, increased class sizes, and increased accountability for student test-performance, many teachers have found meeting the continuum of individual students needs in the regular classroom nearly impossible. Study after study, analysis after anal-ysis on the subject of ability grouping has yielded conflicting information on this complex topic. Yet, most researchers tend to agree that when teachers adjust their curriculum and instruction to the achievement and skill level of the child, students of all achievement levels benefit. This is the approach to achievement grouping that cluster grouping embraces.

Unfortunately, the issues and intricacies surrounding ability grouping have been continually relegated to one side of an ugly argument: ability grouping is either "bad" or "good." Neither could be further from the truth (thus the conflicting results). However, ability grouping is not an easily investigated topic, nor are answers clearly documented. This difficulty is due to the wide range of variables found in the school settings under which ability grouping should be studied if the study is to yield meaningful results. Most teachers know that what goes on within the ability grouping makes it "good" or "bad." The same can be said for whole group instruction, cooperative learning, inclusion, or resource rooms.

Research on tracking has shown that students in higher tracks benefited from this placement, but students in the lower tracks did not (e.g, Slavin, 1987a). Some researchers concluded that placing students in the higher tracks caused the poor achievement of students in lower tracks (Oakes, 1985). Logically, one must question whether this is indeed possible. How could those students not present cause anything?

Might other factors have "caused" the performance in both groups, such as the quality of the teachers, their expectations, or the curriculum? Opinions range from the belief that tracking is the cause of America's failing schools (Oakes, 1985) to conclusions that, without ability grouping, both high and low ability students would be harmed (Kulik, 2003). Renzulli and Reis (1991) explained an important delineation between tracking and ability grouping when they described tracking as "the general and usually permanent assignment of students to classes taught at a certain level," and ability grouping as "a more flexible arrangement that takes into account factors in addition to ability, and sometimes in the place of ability" (p. 31). Even so, research regarding tracking has become generalized to include all forms of ability grouping, though the terms tracking and ability grouping are not synonymous (Tieso, 2003).

GROUPING TERMINOLOGY DEFINITIONS

Because terms surrounding grouping are often attributed with different, conflicting definitions and because these definitions often overlap or carry emotional weight, we provide the following definitions to clarify terms used throughout this book.

General Cluster Grouping

Cluster grouping has a variety of definitions based on how it is implemented, but it can generally be defined as placing several high-achieving, high-ability, or gifted students in a regular classroom with other students and with a teacher who has received training or has a desire to differentiate curriculum and instruction for these "target" students (Gentry, 1999).

Total School Cluster Grouping (as applied by the school in the study referenced in this book)

Total School Cluster Grouping takes General Cluster Grouping several steps further to consider the placement and performance of every student in the school together with the students who might traditionally be identified as gifted and placed in the cluster classroom under the general model. The focus of this book will be on the application of Total School Cluster Grouping, which differs from general clustering in the following important ways:

- ✤ Identification occurs yearly on the basis of student performance, with the expectation that student achievement will increase as students grow, develop, and respond to appropriately differentiated curricula.

* Identification encompasses the range of low-achieving to high-achieving students, with all student achievement levels identified.

* The classroom(s) that contain clusters of high achievers contain no above-average achieving students, as these students are clustered into the other classrooms.

* Some classrooms may contain clusters of special needs students with assistance provided to the classroom teacher.

* Teachers may flexibly group between classes or among grade levels as well as use a variety of flexible grouping strategies within their classrooms.

* All teachers receive professional development in gifted education strategies and have the opportunity for more advanced education in gifted education and talent development through advanced workshops, conferences, and coursework.

* The teacher whose class includes the high-achieving cluster is selected by his or her colleagues and provides differentiated instruction and curriculum to these students as needed to meet their educational needs.

Ability Grouping

Students of similar ability are placed together in groups so that the teacher can modify the pace, instruction, and curriculum to address the needs of individual students who have different abilities in different curricular areas (Tieso, 2003). Kulik (1992) warned, "benefits are slight from programs that group children by ability but prescribe common curricular experiences for all ability groups" (p. 21). He also stressed that students from all ability levels gain when curriculum and instruction are adjusted to meet their learning needs. Ability grouping can be done by subject, within classes, or between classes, and for part of the day or throughout the day. In some applications of ability grouping, the composition of the groups changes while in others it does not.

Achievement Grouping

Similar to ability grouping, achievement grouping focuses on demonstrated levels of achievement by students. Achievement is viewed as something dynamic and changing. Like ability grouping, achievement or skill level grouping can be done by subject, within or between classes, part of the day or all day. It very often takes place in a flexible manner as performance and achievement levels of students change (Renzulli & Reis, 1997). Throughout this book we use the term "achievement grouping" rather than the term "ability grouping" due to its more fluid and manifest definition. Ability is often equated to intelligence and viewed as latent and fixed, whereas achievement is more likely to be viewed as changeable or to be affected by effective educational opportunities. It must also be noted that high achievers inherently have high ability, whereas not all high-ability students are high achievers.

Between-class Grouping

This type of grouping occurs when students are regrouped for a subject area (usually within an elementary grade level) based on ability or achievement. Teachers instruct students working at similar levels with appropriately challenging curricula, at an appropriate pace, and with methods most suited to facilitate academic gain. For example, in mathematics one teacher may be teaching algebra to advanced students, while a colleague teaches pre-algebra to students not as advanced, and yet another teacher works with students for whom math is a struggle, employing strategies to enhance their success and understanding. Between-class grouping arrangements by subject areas usually require that grade-level teachers teach the subject at the same time to facilitate the grouping arrangements.

Within-class Grouping

Within-class grouping refers to different arrangements teachers use within their classes. Groups may be created by interest, skill, achievement, job, ability, self-selection—either heterogeneous or homogeneous—and can include various forms of cooperative-learning grouping arrangements. Flexible arrangements for within-class grouping are desirable.

Tracking

Tracking is full-time placement of students into ability groups for instruction—usually by class and at the secondary level. In a tracked system, there is very little opportunity to move between the various tracks, and placement in the tracks is often determined by some form of "objective" testing. Tracking is "the practice of grouping students according to their perceived abilities . . . the groups are sometimes labeled college bound, academic, vocational, general, and remedial" (McBrien & Brandt, 1997, pp. 97-98). Tracking has very little to do with ability or achievement grouping in elementary grades, although it has often been generalized to elementary school settings and used to discourage grouping with young children.

Flexible Grouping

Flexible grouping calls for using various forms of grouping for instruction, pacing, and curricula in a manner that allows for student movement between and within groups based on their progress and needs. Flexible grouping takes place (a) when there is more than one form of grouping used (class, project, job, skill, heterogeneous, homogeneous) and (b) when group membership, in some or all of these groups, changes according to the form of grouping used. Keep in mind that groups are formed and modified based on the academic needs of the students. Both critics and supporters of grouping agree that grouping should be flexible (Gentry, 1999; George, 1995; Renzulli & Reis, 1997; Slavin, 1987b).

Table 1.1 summarizes the grouping terminology definitions.

ABILITY GROUPING CONSIDERATIONS

Slavin (1987b, 1990, 2006) listed three important advantages of regrouping students for selected subjects over homogeneous ability grouped class assignments: (a) identifying and placing students in the setting for most of the day reduces labeling effects, (b) achievement in reading or math determines group placement—not ability level, and (c) regrouping plans tend to be flexible. In their meta-analyses, Kulik and Kulik (1991) reported that within-class programs specifically designed to benefit gifted and talented students raised the achievement scores of these students. Slavin (1987a) reported that within-class ability grouping had a positive effect (.34 standard deviations) on the mathematics achievements of all students, with the most positive effect for students who initially achieved at low levels. He also stated that the within-class use of grouping for reading instruction might be necessary. After reviewing the effects of 13 different research syntheses on grouping, Rogers (1991, 2002) concluded that grouping students on the basis of academic ability and on the basis of general intellectual ability has "produced marked academic achievement gains as well as moderate increases in attitude toward the subjects in which these students are grouped" (1991, p. xii). Despite many arguments for and against ability grouping, it appears from reviews of the research that grouping can help to improve the academic performance of students of all achievement levels if implemented with appropriate curriculum, instruction, and expectations.

For grouping to positively affect the academic achievement of students, more than a simple administrative grouping plan must exist. As demonstrated by the

Table 1.1. Grouping Terminology.

Term	Definition
Cluster Grouping	The placement of several high-achieving, high-ability, or gifted students in a regular classroom with other students and a teacher who has received training or has a desire to differentiate curriculum and instruction for these "target" students.
Total School Cluster Grouping	Cluster grouping model that takes into account the achievement levels of all students and places students in classrooms yearly in order to reduce the number of achievement levels in each classroom and facilitate teachers' differentiation of curriculum and instruction for all students and thus increase student achievement.
Ability Grouping	Students are grouped for the purpose of modification of pace, instruction, and curriculum. Groups can be flexible and arranged by subject, within classes, or between classes.
Achievement Grouping	Focuses on demonstrated levels of achievement by students and is viewed as something dynamic and changing. Groups can be arranged by subject, within classes, or between classes.
Between-class Grouping	Students are regrouped for a subject area (usually within an elementary grade level) based on ability or achievement. Teachers instruct students working at similar levels with appropriately challenging curricula, at an appropriate pace, and with methods most suited to facilitate academic gain.
Within-class Grouping	These groups are different arrangements teachers use within their classes. Groups may be created by interest, skill, achievement, job, ability, self-selection—either heterogeneous or homogeneous—and can include various forms of cooperative learning grouping arrangements. Groups are intended to be flexible.
Tracking	The full-time placement of students into ability groups for instruction, usually by class and at the secondary level. Little opportunity exists to move between tracks.
Flexible Grouping	The use of various forms of grouping for instruction, pacing, and curriculum in such a manner to allow for movement of students between and among groups based on their progress and needs

varied results from the meta-analytic studies on grouping, there is more to grouping than simply assigning students to groups on the basis of their ability or achievement levels. Rogers (1991) suggested it was unlikely grouping itself caused the gains. The studies that reported the largest effects were of programs that provided differentiation within ability groups (Kulik, 1992, 2003; Rogers, 1991, 2002). Kulik (2003) noted that bright, average, and low-achieving youngsters benefited from grouping programs if the curriculum was appropriately adjusted to the aptitude levels of the groups. Accordingly, he recommended schools use various forms of flexible ability grouping. In discussing their meta-analyses findings on grouping practices, Kulik and Kulik (1992) concluded:

> If schools eliminated grouping programs with differentiated curricula, the damage to student achievement would be great, and it would be felt broadly. Both higher and lower aptitude students would suffer academically from the elimination of such programs. The damage would be truly great if, in the name of de-tracking, schools eliminated enriched and accelerated classes for their brightest learners. The achievement level of such students would fall dramatically if they were required to move at the common pace. No one can be certain that there would be a way to repair the harm that would be done. (p. 73)

WHAT THE RESEARCH SAYS ABOUT CLUSTER GROUPING

It is clear that a discrepancy exists between what takes place in schools for students with regard to challenge and instructional strategies and what should take place if American students are to compete in a global marketplace (Renzulli, 2005). Restricting the range of student achievement levels in classrooms results in more time for teachers to work with individual students. Cluster grouping has been found to be beneficial to students in that it allows students of similar achievement levels to work together and challenge each other. For high-ability learners, cluster grouping also allows them the opportunity to compare themselves to their intellectual peers and form a more accurate perception of their own abilities. By not always being best or first academically, they learn to work, to fail, to strive for excellence, and they have others' high quality work with which to compare their own work. These elements are essential for high-ability students to learn to work to their potential (Robinson, Reis, Neihart, & Moon, 2002).

Researchers have noted numerous benefits from grouping gifted students. These benefits include improved academic achievement (Gentry, 1999; Tieso, 2005), realistic perception of abilities when compared to peers (Marsh, Chessor, Craven, & Roche, 1995), appropriate levels of challenge (Kulik, 2003; Rogers, 2002), the ability for teachers to address unique social and emotional needs of gifted students (Peterson, 2003), and the ability for teachers to better address individual strengths and weakness with a more focused range of ability levels (Moon, 2003). Additionally, research indicates that there are several major benefits to cluster grouping:

* Gifted students regularly interact both with their intellectual peers and their age peers (Delcourt & Evans, 1994; Rogers, 1991; Slavin, 1987a).

* Cluster grouping provides full-time services for gifted students without additional cost (Gentry & Owen, 1999; Hoover, Sayler, & Feldhusen, 1993; LaRose, 1986).

* Curricular differentiation is more effective and likely to occur when a group of high-achieving students is placed with a teacher who has expertise, training, and a desire to differentiate curriculum than when these students are distributed among many teachers (Bryant, 1987; Kennedy, 1995; Kulik, 1992; Rogers, 2002).

* Removing the highest achievers from most classrooms allows other achievers to emerge and gain recognition (Gentry & Owen, 1999; Kennedy, 1989).

* Student achievement increases when cluster grouping is used (Brulles, 2005; Gentry & Owen, 1999; Pierce, Cassady, Adams, Dixon, Speirs Neumeister, & Cross, 2007).

* Over time, fewer students are identified as low achievers and more students are identified as high achievers (Gentry, 1999).

* Cluster grouping reduces the range of student achievement levels that must be addressed within the classrooms of all teachers (Coleman, 1995; Gentry, 1999; Delcourt & Evans 1994; Rogers, 1993).

Several analyses of studies regarding ability grouping in elementary schools have been completed (Kulik, 1992; Kulik & Kulik, 1984, 1985, 1992; Lou, Abrami, Spence, Poulsen, Chambers, & d'Apollonia, 1996; Rogers, 1991; Slavin, 1987a); however, only ten published studies could be found that examined the effects of ability grouping on gifted students in schools where a cluster grouping model was used (Delcourt & Evans, 1994; Delcourt, Loyd, Cornell, & Goldberg, 1994; Gentry, 1999; Gentry & Owen, 1999; Hoover, Sayler, & Feldhusen, 1993; Ivey, 1965; LaRose, 1986; Long 1957; Ziehl, 1962). Eight of these studies were concerned with the effects of cluster grouping on gifted students, and only our work examined effects on students of other achievement levels.

Although cluster grouping is commonly suggested as a programming option for gifted students, surprisingly little evidence exists regarding its effects on these students. A single study examined the effects of cluster grouping on all students and on teachers' perceptions of other students' performance (Gentry & Owen, 1999). Gentry (1999) and Gentry & Owen (1999) reported that for two entire classes (i.e., graduation years) of students, when compared to similar students in a longitudinal, quasi-experimental study, student achievement increased among all students in the cluster-grouped school. Standardized achievement scores in math, reading, and the total battery on the Iowa Tests of Basic Skills (Hieronymus, Hoover, & Lindquist, 1984) improved for two entire graduation years between grades two and five. Further, the cluster-grouped students began with lower total achievement than their comparison school counter parts for each graduation year of students and ended with significantly higher total achievement than the comparison school students. These achievement trends are depicted in Figures 1.1 and 1.2. The gains in achievement

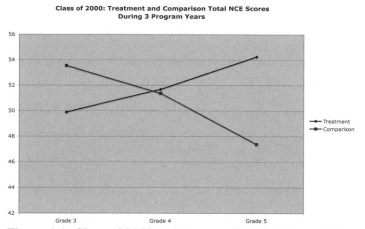

Figure 1.1. Class of 2000 treatment and comparison NCE scores during 3-program years.

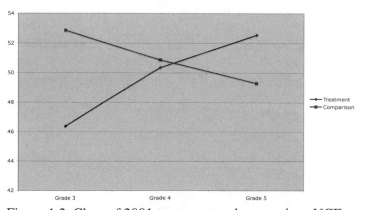

Figure 1.2. Class of 2001 treatment and comparison NCE scores during 3 program years.

and the differences in achievement were both statistically and practically significant with medium to large effect sizes.

Additionally, more students in the treatment school were identified as above average or high achievers while fewer students were identified as low achievers during the 5-year span of the study. Changes in the achievement categories are depicted in Figures 1.3 and 1.4. Gentry (1999) also reported qualitative findings concerning teacher practices, administrative leadership, and the various uses of grouping that helped to explain the achievement and identification findings.

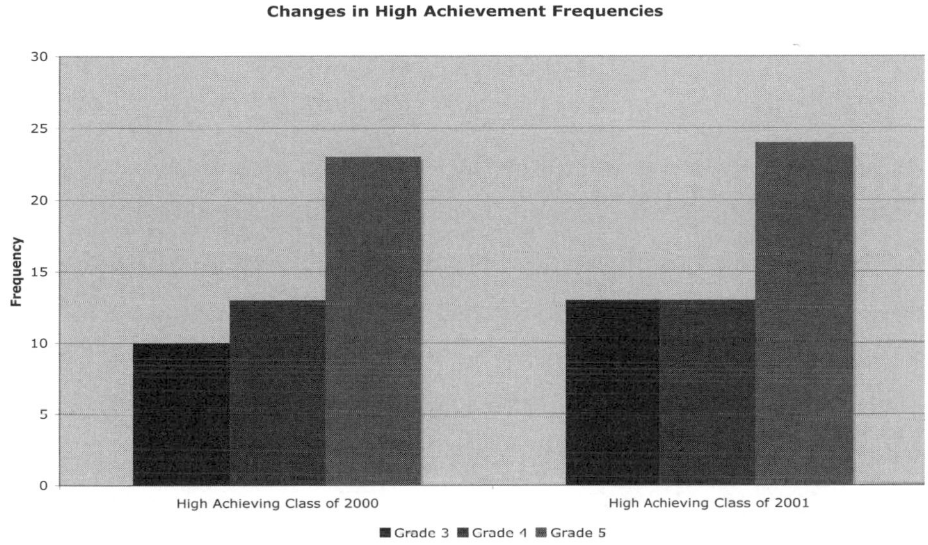

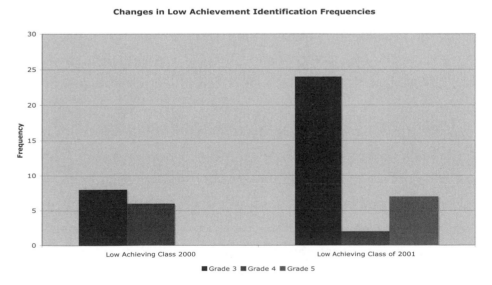

Figure 1.3. Changes in frequencies of identified high-achieving students during 3 program years.

Figure 1.4. Changes in frequencies of identified low-achieving students during 3 program years.

Since this research was published, this model has been widely recommended and implemented, but most districts show little interest in publishing the results of their efforts, hence only anecdotal information exists concerning the efficacy of implementation in these varied sites (e.g., Teno, 2000). However, this study has been replicated with similar findings reported in dissertation format (Brulles, 2005) and in conference proceedings (Pierce et al., 2007), and we are currently engaged in a longitudinal replication study in Indiana. The Total School Cluster Grouping Model that we studied in the mid-1990s and that we are currently replicating serves as the conceptual basis for the remainder of this book.

TOTAL SCHOOL CLUSTER GROUPING

Total School Cluster Grouping operates on the premise that the gifted education program will enhance the entire school. As noted by Tomlinson and Callahan (1992), Renzulli (1994), Reis, Gentry, and Park (1995), and the U.S. Department of Education (1993), the use of gifted education "know-how" has the potential to improve general education practices. The long-term study conducted by Gubbins and the NRC/GT Research Team (2002) found that by employing strategies typically used in gifted programs, academic needs were more likely to become the focus of the curriculum than the typical themed units (watermelons, apples, pumpkins) that had previously presided in many classrooms. Cluster grouping, when designed appropriately, can simultaneously address the needs of high-achieving students and the needs of other students.

The professional development component of this model had positive effects not only on the students, but the teachers also felt that they received both the instructional and collegial support that allowed them to become leaders in their schools (Gentry & Keilty, 2004). Due to the total-school effects of cluster grouping, professional development plays a critical role in the model's success. On-going staff development opportunities afforded teachers opportunities to explore instructional strategies that can be implemented successfully in cluster-grouped classrooms. Through integrating higher-order thinking skills, developing critical thinking skills, compacting curriculum, using open-ended questions, accelerating students in content areas, and using several other instructional strategies, teachers reported being able to address the specific needs of their students (Gentry & Owen, 1999). According to Teacher 3A (a third grade teacher who taught the high-achieving cluster students):

> We had so many high [achieving] math students who weren't in a cluster [for high-achieving students]. We thought, to really meet the needs of the grade level, we would have a cluster group strictly for math. We also had the high [achieving] cluster reading group to meet the needs of other children who may not have been identified or who had strengths that weren't evident across the board. We were able to target more children for high reading by regrouping within the grade level for reading. (p. 234)

The focus on the individual abilities and needs of students in the cluster groups provided more opportunities to identify students at higher levels. For example, Teacher 4C (who taught a fourth-grade class) explained:

> Maybe cluster grouping has a lot to do with it. The cluster grouping may give the lower-achieving students more self-confidence . . . I think they become more involved in class when the high [achieving] kids are removed. And you know that those high [achieving] kids are competitive and tend to dominate class sometimes. Also, the average student or high-average student really blossomed, too, which may be due to cluster grouping. (Gentry & Owen, 1999, pp.228-229)

Kulik and Kulik (1992) and Rogers (1991) suggested that grouping by ability, when used in conjunction with appropriate differentiated instruction, can be beneficial to the achievement of all students. When placed together, gifted students are given the opportunity to see the level at which their academic peers are performing. While in heterogeneous groups, these students may be able to perform at a sub-par level and still be seen as excelling beyond their classmates, when in truth they are capable of so much more (Kulik, 2003; Rogers, 2002). By grouping more homogeneously, the façade of effort and ability can be removed and replaced with more appropriate challenge and rigor.

In turn, the same phenomenon occurs in the other classrooms. Students who previously sat quietly, able to avoid participation, are now free to engage in and contribute to the learning process. As expectations are raised for all students, accountability increases, attention focuses, and productivity begins to increase. By regrouping the student population according to achievement levels, educators are better able to meet both the diverse needs of the students and the non-negotiable restrictions of the budget (Gentry, 1999).

Administrators and teachers noted the merit of Total School Cluster Grouping, as it provided positive results for both teachers and students. The teachers liked the program, and 95% of them believed it helped them better meet the needs of the students in their classrooms (Gentry, 1999). One teacher explained how she came to view the program:

> One thing—I remember how skeptical I was at the beginning because I am not a risk-taker. I thought the same thing a few other people thought—oh, you take those top kids out and I'm not going to have any spark. And that was far from being true. I see lots of sparks in my room. . . . And having my daughter in [the program], . . . there's such a difference in her attitude and her love for school is back. . . . Before being placed in the high-achieving cluster, she wasn't being challenged in school, now to see her doing research projects as an eight-year-old. . . . She's doing projects so beyond what I ever thought, and she is so excited about school. (p. 238)

In summary Total School Cluster Grouping is a model with a growing body of research. Its use has the potential to meet the academic needs of gifted and talented students and to help all students achieve at high levels. In the next chapter we discuss Total School Cluster Grouping in detail.

2

TOTAL SCHOOL CLUSTER GROUPING MODEL: IMPLEMENTATION & PRACTICE

The Total School Cluster Grouping Model provides an organizational framework that places students into classrooms on the basis of achievement, flexibly groups and regroups students as needed for instruction (based on interests and needs), and provides appropriately challenging learning experiences for all students. This chapter describes the details and considerations necessary for successfully implementing the Total School Cluster Grouping Model.

IDENTIFICATION

Identification is a key component for all programming, and in Total School Cluster Grouping, formal identification takes place yearly, with the expectation that students will improve over time in their achievement performance. Criteria are not fixed, but rather determined by consensus that includes the flexibility to accommodate individual students and their needs. In addition to yearly identification and placement of students, the model includes flexible grouping and regrouping of students for instruction once they are placed in classrooms. Following are the general categories of achievement that facilitate yearly identification for classroom placement.

Categories of Achievement

Identification in a traditional gifted program can be fraught with problems of accountability, testing, elitism, equity, and limited space in the program. These issues do not pose problems in the Total School Cluster Grouping Model. The achievement levels of all students are identified using a combination of student performance in the classroom as identified by their teachers and achievement test results. Every year students are identified as belonging in one of five categories.

The Five Achievement Categories

1. <u>High Achieving:</u> These students are great at math *and* reading when compared to their age peers.

2. <u>Above-Average Achieving</u>: These students are great at math *or* reading, or they are pretty good at math and reading, but not as advanced at both as students identified as high achieving.

3. <u>Average Achieving</u>: These students achieve in the middle when compared to others in their grade level. Their achievement might be "on grade level" in many schools. In an impoverished area, they might be achieving below grade level, but at an average level for the school population.

4. <u>Low-Average Achieving</u>: These students may struggle with math or reading, or be slightly behind their peers in both areas. However, it also appears, that with some extra support, these students are not at risk of failure.

5. <u>Low Achieving</u>: These students struggle with school and face risk of failure in school. In many schools the longer they attend, the further behind they fall. These are the students for whom school seems to fail.

Another category could be developed for special needs students. However these students have already been identified, so placing them where they can succeed becomes the only concern. To facilitate this placement, the achievement levels of these students should be noted. Many students served by special education are not low achieving, and they should never be assumed to be low-achieving students. Many students may have more than one label, such as ADHD and gifted or LD and gifted. If a student has a dual exceptionality, educators should place the student in the high-achieving cluster, so that the twice-exceptional student's strengths can be the educational focus.

Teachers, counselors, and administrators need to understand these identification category definitions and that the categories are based on the population attending their school. By using a local frame of reference, the system of identification can work in any type of school. If a school is "average" (is there such a school?), then an average student would be on grade level, whereas if a school is high performing an average student might be achieving above grade level. These categories are based on relative performance. The *Scales for Rating the Behavioral Characteristics of Superior Students* (Renzulli, Smith, White, Callahan, Hartman, &Westberg, 2002) might assist teachers in understanding characteristics of academically high-performing students, though the ratings should never be summed and used in an identification matrix. It is also important to understand that

    ⁂ identification categories are designed to assist with student placement in this model, not as definitive, permanent labels, or as indicators of expectations;

⁂ categories change as students grow, learn, and develop, so that a specific identification category might not drive instructional placement for students identified in average, low-average, or low achieving categories; and

⁂ identification takes place yearly for classroom placement, and students will likely improve as they progress through school.

Identification Procedures and Guidelines

Once these categories are established and explained, the process of identifying the achievement levels of students for placement in classrooms can begin. This process is labor intensive and involves several steps. First, we try to have teachers identify the performance of their students prior to examining any test performance data. The order in the process is important as both the teacher designations and the test performance will be used to identify and place students in the classrooms. If teachers check the tests to see if they are "right," and then adjust their assessments of student achievement based on test results, the information used for placement will have too much test emphasis rather than a balance of information from both teachers and test results. This model uses tests for means of inclusion into the program, not for means of exclusion from the program, as do so many other identification systems.

Teacher assessments will identify students who fail to test well, but who perform well in class. Teachers, in general, know their students. Occasionally, teachers will fail to identify as gifted (or high achieving) students who fail to do their work, who are unorganized, or who are defiant. There are many reasons for not identifying this type of student, not the least of which is that such a child might take a spot away from a more "deserving" child. In this model, there is no limit to the number of spaces in the high-achieving cluster. If a child scores well on the test, but does not perform well in class, he or she will be placed in the high-achieving cluster by merit of his or her test scores, thus the test is used to include students who teachers might not otherwise identify for placement. We suggest using a local norm of 90th to 95th percentile in both math and reading for automatic inclusion into the high-achieving cluster. Other high achievers will be so designated by their teachers regardless of their test scores. In the event of a teacher who over-nominates, have that teacher rank the nominated students in order of greatest need.

To include students as above-average achieving, educators can use a local norm of 90th to 95th percentile in math *or* reading or 75th percentile in math *and* reading. Again, teachers will include others who exhibit (but do not test with) above-average performance.

By using both teacher ratings and achievement scores, a system of checks and balances is developed. Through this method it is possible for a student who didn't test well to be identified, and conversely, a student whose classroom performance did not reflect his or her ability could be identified as high achieving or above average on the basis of achievement scores. Due to the holistic approach and flexible nature of this identification process, cut-off scores and matrices should not be employed. The use of cut-off scores may cause educators to misidentify students by placing too much emphasis on one factor. Using a matrix focuses on a combination of rigid factors rather than fluid pathways to identification. Students are simply identified and placed into classes by the people who know them best and have their best interests in mind.

Other Considerations

When teachers designate the achievement levels of their students, so too, should they designate which students need to be separated from each other, which students have behavior problems, and specific students who receive special assistance in areas such as math, reading, language, speech, etc. If parent requests for placing children in particular classrooms are usually honored, it needs to be made clear, for reasons forthcoming (see Developing Class Lists and Reaching Out to Parents), that placement might not be possible.

Student Data Cards: An Example from Practice

Participants at our current study site have developed a Student Data Card based on these identification procedures, and they have found the cards to work quite effectively. Teachers use the cards to record all the information pertinent to placement and bring the completed cards to a grade-level placement conference. A sample Student Data Card is depicted in Figure 2.1. This card can be adapted for use in other districts based on local information and placement considerations.

DEVELOPING CLASS LISTS

The information gathered in the identification process is used to develop draft class lists for the following school year. Teachers have used Student Data Cards, index cards, or sticky notes with all the information on each student included on the card. Teachers can stick them to a wall, table, or door and easily move them among the classes until an ideal solution is reached by the grade-level team. Other teachers

Student Data Summary Card

School Year:

Name: Current Grade: Projected Grade:

Gender: M   F   Race:

	Language Arts	Math	Science
State Test			
NWEA			

Final Reading Grade:

Final Math Grade:

Running Record A-Z:

Identification Category (circle one):

High Achieving   Above Average   Average   Low Average   Low

Special Education (achievement level):

English Proficiency Level: 1   2   3   4   5   N/A

Discipline Issues:	Never	Seldom	Often
Attendance Issues:	Never	Seldom	Often

Other Comments:

Figure 2.1. Sample student data card.

have computerized the information, and still other educators simply work from a printed class list. Whatever the method in developing class lists, the goals of the process are to

- reduce the number of achievement groups that each teacher has in his or her classroom while still maintaining some heterogeneity,
- cluster the high-achieving students in one classroom,
- place a group of above-average students in each of the remaining teacher's classrooms,
- cluster students needing special services in classrooms (if appropriate) with resource personnel assistance,
- honor parental requests for specific teachers when possible and if it follows building or district policy,
- evenly distribute behavior problems among all classrooms so that no teacher has more than his or her fair share of difficult students, and
- involve teachers in developing the class lists.

Using these goals as a guide, an administrator, secretary, counselor, or coordinator can begin to develop the draft class lists. Once the drafts are completed, the current grade-level teachers and an administrator or coordinator should sit down and review the lists with the above goals in mind. During this placement conference, which can initially take an hour or two, the teachers (who know both their colleagues and their students) should review the lists for appropriateness. Teachers should feel free to suggest and make student placement changes. The only rule concerning moving students is that like-labeled students must be "traded" among the classrooms. For example, an average student from Classroom A can be traded for an average student from Classroom B to create a better student-teacher fit. An average student cannot be traded for an above-average, below-average, or any other category student. Once all the changes have been made, the lists can be finalized.

We recommend using an asterisk to highlight any student who is placed in a classroom for a specific reason. The asterisk denotes that the student may not be moved. When a request for change is made (usually to someone in the office), the person taking the request can quickly glance at the class lists and easily move unasterisked students in the same identification categories. If a request comes in for a change that would require moving an asterisked student, we recommend that school personnel tell the parent or guardian that making a change is not currently an option, but that it would be possible to revisit the request after four to six weeks of school. Usually, the student will acclimate to the class during that time period. If after four to six weeks of school, the placement is not working for the student, a change should be considered. (For more on this topic, see Reaching Out to Parents.)

By using these procedures for placing students into classrooms each year, the goals for developing the classes can be met. Tables 2.1-2.4 depict how the placement might look for a particular grade level in a school with two to five classrooms per grade level. If the number of classrooms exceeds five per grade level, then teachers can consider designating two classrooms per grade level in which to place high-achieving students. In large schools of ten or more classrooms per grade level, three or more high-achieving cluster classrooms might be needed. Please keep in mind that the number of high-achieving students will vary from year to year, as will the numbers of student in all achievement categories. Since the model's goal is to enhance the achievement of more students over time, it can accommodate any number of high achievers.

As students progress through the grade levels and as teachers identify more students who begin to achieve at higher levels, it may be necessary to add additional classrooms to accommodate the increased numbers of high-achieving students. By grade five in our study school, teachers faced a decision about whether to have one self-contained classroom of high-achievers or to have two classrooms with clusters of high-achieving students. Such a situation presents a positive problem in a school: what to do with all of the students who achieve at such high levels? In this school the fifth-grade team of teachers discussed the situation and decided to have one teacher teach all of the high-achieving students, thus creating a self-contained class in the fifth-grade. Had there been another fifth-grade teacher who wanted a cluster of high-achieving students, they could have just as easily decided to create two cluster classrooms in grade five. Each solution would have worked. We should note that the other four classrooms each had a large number of above-average students and a small number of low-achieving students, as student achievement had increased during the three program years.

As displayed in Tables 2.1-2.4, the range of ability levels has been significantly reduced from what one would likely find in a typical heterogeneous classroom that was computer generated or in a classroom in which the students were distributed evenly in order to be "fair" to the teachers. In this model, we recognize that having a similar number of different types of students in classrooms is not fair: it creates too wide a range of achievement levels for teachers to effectively meet the diverse needs of their individual students. The reduction in the range of achievement levels allows for a more focused and academically appropriate curricular approach, thus increasing the chances that individual students' academic needs will be met.

Table 2.1. Third-grade Students Grouped Into Five Classrooms.

ID Category	Room 1	Room 2	Room 3	Room 4	Room 5	3rd-grade Total
High-achieving	11	0	0	0	0	11
Above-average	0	7	7	7	7	28
Average	8	8	8	8	8	40
Low-average	4	4	2	4	6	20
Low	0	6	6	4	0	16
Special Education	2*	0	2	2	4**	10
Total	25	25	25	25	25	125

*These students are Learning Disabled *and* Gifted.
**These students are Learning Disabled and see the same teacher consultant who spends 4 half-days per week working in this classroom.

Table 2.2. Second-grade Students Grouped Into Four Classrooms.

ID Category	Room 1	Room 2	Room 3	Room 4	2nd-grade Total
High-achieving	8	0	0	0	8
Above-average	0	7	7	7	21
Average	10	10	10	10	40
Low-average	5	0	5	5	15
Low	0	8	0	3	11
Special Education	2*	0	3**	0	5
Total	25	25	25	25	100

*These students are Learning Disabled *and* Gifted.
**These students see the same teacher consultant who also helps the classroom teacher.

Table 2.3. Fourth-grade Students Grouped Into Three Classrooms.

ID Category	Room 1	Room 2	Room 3	4th-grade Total
High-achieving	6	0	0	6
Above-average	0	7	6	13
Average	10	10	10	30
Low-average	8	0	6	14
Low	0	8	0	8
Special Education	1*	0	3**	4
Total	25	25	25	75

*This student is twice-exceptional.
**These students see the same teacher consultant who also helps the classroom teacher.

Table 2.4. Fifth-grade Students Grouped Into Two Classrooms.

ID Category	Room 1	Room 2	5th-grade Total
High-achieving	6	0	6
Above-average	0	7	7
Average	10	10	20
Low-average	7	0	7
Low	0	6	6
Special Education*	2	2	4
Total	25	25	50

*Placement of special education students is done based on individual students' needs.

As noted in the Tables 2.1-2.4, a cluster of students with learning disabilities exists in one classroom, and that classroom teacher receives assistance. This manner of inclusion brings the special education teacher into the classroom, integrating her into the general education classroom. The students who receive special services are, in effect, clustered as well, and this arrangement affords them a peer group rather than singling them out as the only kid in class who is different and who receives special services. In turn, the special education teacher is a master of differentiation and can help ensure that methods and materials are appropriate for the varied achievement levels of the students. Whether to cluster special needs students is a district decision.

It should be noted that each year presents a new continuum of student needs. Some years will seem "normal" in their distribution of students achieving at various levels (e.g., a few students at each end of the normal curve and most students near the center). Other years may present quite a different situation such as those depicted in Tables 2.5 and 2.6 on the following page. These tables contain actual data from a school in which the numbers of students at the various achievement levels did not follow a normal distribution. The school depicted in Table 2.5 had an unusually high number of both high and low achievers. Teachers agreed at the placement conference to reduce the number of students in Classroom 5 to help this teacher attend to a large cluster of low-achieving students. The special education teacher worked beside the teacher in this classroom and helped her differentiate for the special education students. In addition, this teacher had full-time services from a Title 1 aide. Because she had only two achievement levels, she was able to provide differentiated services to both groups of students.

Table 2.6 shows three first-grade classrooms. Due to the make-up of this grade level, each teacher's class has two achievement levels, rather than the more common range of five achievement levels. This arrangement should make planning, teaching, and differentiation easier for these three teachers. In this example no children had yet been identified for special education services, hence their absence from the table.

Note that in these situations, some teachers only had two distinct achievement groups in their classrooms. Be flexible as you place students after assessing the numbers of students who achieve at the different levels in the entire grade. A unique aspect of the Total School Cluster Grouping Model is that there are no preconceived notions about how many students can or must be identified as "gifted."

Admittedly, time and energy are involved in identifying students and developing class lists. The payoff occurs in the following year in the classroom when each teacher can more effectively reach his or her students due to the decrease in

Table 2.5. Third-grade Students Grouped Into Five Classrooms: Atypical Year.

ID Category	Room 1	Room 2	Room 3	Room 4	Room 5	3rd-grade Total
High-achieving	10	10	0	0	0	20
Above-average	0	0	7	7	7	21
Average	0	8	8	8	0	24
Low-average	16	0	0	9	0	25
Low	0	6	10	0	10	26
Special Education	0	2*	0	2	4**	8
Total	26	26	25	26	21	124

*These students are Learning Disabled *and* Gifted.
** These students are Learning Disabled and see the same teacher consultant who spends 4 half-days per week working in this classroom; the teacher consultant will work in the classroom with the teacher. Her class size has been reduced.

Table 2.6. First-grade Students Grouped Into Three Classrooms: Atypical Year.

ID Category	Room 1	Room 2	Room 3	1st-grade Total
High-achieving	6	0	0	6
Above-average	0	5	5	10
Average	14	0	0	14
Low-average	0	15	0	15
Low	0	0	15	15
Special Education	0	0	0	0
Total	20	20	20	60

the number of achievement levels in each classroom (facilitating more efficient use of differentiation strategies). A realistic timeline for identifying and making placements is depicted in Table 2.7. Some districts set aside an afternoon for placement conferences, others hold these conferences after school or during a staff meeting time slot, and still others have used common grade-level planning time. One school in our current study has teachers from all grade levels sit at tables in the cafeteria during a half-day professional development time (provided as required by state law). Such an arrangement facilitates discussion about students both within and among the various grade levels.

Table 2.7. Sample Timeline for Identifying and Placing Students.

When	Action	Time
Late Spring	Teachers complete identification using the 5 categories	1-2 hours within a 1-2 week window of time
Late Spring	Coordinator or administrator develops draft class lists	2-4 hours
Late Spring	Teachers have placement conferences and finalize lists	1-3 hours

Placing New Students After School Starts

All schools receive new students at the beginning of the school year, but occasionally students enroll mid-semester or mid-year. Because records often take several days to reach new schools, resulting in an absence of information about the academic skills of a new student, we suggest conducting a quick assessment of reading and math skills when new students enroll. Educators can then place new students tentatively into classrooms until records arrive and student performance can be more fully assessed. Teachers should explain to parents or guardians that the initial classroom placement is temporary and that a permanent placement will be made within two or three weeks. In the vast majority of the cases, the initial placement will work just fine. In cases of extremely low or high achievement, a move might be warranted.

TEACHER SELECTION AND APPOINTMENT

One perceived challenge in the initial implementation of a Total School Cluster Grouping Program might involve which teachers teach which classrooms of students. In examining schools that have implemented cluster grouping, we have recognized some basic "truths" concerning how to select and appoint educators to teach the high achieving (and other) cluster classrooms.

First, the teacher in the high-achieving classroom must want to work with these students and commit to differentiating the curriculum to provide these students with appropriately challenging curriculum and instruction. Second, this individual must commit to learning about how to work with these students through coursework, workshops, licensure, or degree programs. Third, if selected to teach this classroom, the appointment is not a lifetime appointment, but it will last for a minimum of three years. Three years provides the teacher with a first year to learn how to facilitate the high-achieving students, a second year to perfect it, and a third year to enjoy it. Of course, during those three years, if a teachers finds that this assignment is not his or her strength or if someone leaves the position, another interested teacher can fill the position. At the end of three years, the appointment will be revisited in the context of the grade level and consideration will be given to other teachers who have an interest in working with high-achieving students. We recommend a rotating appointment to offer others the opportunity to teach the high-achieving students and to reduce the appearance of exclusivity. However, change at the end of three years occurs only if another teacher wants the opportunity and commits to the training.

In this model, if implemented as described, more students are likely to be identified each year as talented; thus the demand for teachers to work with high-achieving students will increase over time. Further, districts that implement between-class grouping in math and/or reading will need more teachers who have the desire and skills to teach the high-achieving cluster, high-achieving math group, and high-achieving reading group. The high-achieving cluster teacher need not also teach both advanced math and advanced reading. In fact, by involving more than one teacher at each grade level in the delivery of advanced instruction and content, more teachers will develop skills in working with high-achieving students and perceptions of one class as the advanced class are diminished.

We suggest establishing some parameters and an application processes for initially designating teachers who will teach the high-achieving cluster classrooms. These would include knowledge and background, experience and skills, and willingness to engage in additional educational training concerning gifted child education. One district used the simple application depicted in Figure 2.2 to document teacher interest in teaching this cluster classroom.

We also suggest that grade-level teachers sit together and discuss openly who is interested in teaching this classroom. Often the grade-level educators can work together to make the designation. If they do, such a discussion can avoid the appearance of special treatment or questions surrounding the process of who was selected and why he or she was chosen to teach this classroom. Buy-in to the classroom assignment by one's colleagues increases the chances for success and reduces misperceptions and jealousy. Further, once a teacher has a classroom containing a cluster of high-achievers, we recommend that grade levels meet on a regular basis to discuss and plan together. We also recommend that the teacher of the high-achieving cluster be candid with his or her colleagues about exactly how hard he or she works to keep up with the high achievers. Occasionally, perceptions exist that

---

APPLICATION FOR TEACHER OF HIGH ACHIEVEMENT STUDENT GROUP

Name _____

Detail your experience working with high-achieving students.

_____
_____
_____
_____
_____
_____
_____

List relevant education and background in working with high-achieving students (include course-work, workshops, conferences, degrees, certifications, etc).

_____
_____
_____
_____
_____
_____
_____

Grade levels you are willing to teach: K   1   2   3   4   5   6

Are you willing to wait 3 years for this appointment?   Yes   No
If yes, during the time before the appointment, what actions would you take to increase your knowledge in this area?

_____
_____
_____
_____

Explain why teaching this group of students interests you.

_____
_____
_____
_____

Figure 2.2. Sample teacher application.

the high achievers are easy and well-behaved students. However, these perceptions are far from the truth. It would be a mistake for the teacher of the high achievers to give the impression that he or she has all the great kids and that he or she is having a delightful year, when in fact, he or she is likely working harder than ever before.

Ideally, some teachers on staff will have certification or licensure and experience in working with gifted or high-achieving students. Frequently, this case is not the reality. In selecting educators to teach the high achievers, the first criterion needs to be willingness to engage with these students, followed closely by a willingness to obtain expertise about working with these kids. If licensure or certification exists in the state, then the teacher should be given a window of time in which to obtain it. Obtaining expertise need not be dictated simply by what exists in a geographic region, although many areas around the country have on-campus degree or licensure programs in gifted education and talent development. Purdue University offers its licensure courses (a series of five, three-credit, courses) on-line and at reasonable in-state tuition rates for all distance education students (www. purdue.edu/geri), and the University of Connecticut offers a Master's degree in gifted education on-line (www.gifted.uconn.edu). The National Association for Gifted Children (www.nagc.org) has Professional Achievement Certificates in which teachers develop a personal growth plan to gain expertise in working with high-achieving children. Most states offer state conferences in the area of gifted education, and several top-quality summer institutes provide in-depth study in gifted education (e.g., the University of Connecticut's Confratute [www.gifted. uconn.edu], Purdue University's DISCOVER! [www.geri.education.purdue.edu], and Boise State University's Edufest [www.edufest.org]).

If more educators want to teach high-achieving clusters than classrooms exist, we suggest encouraging expertise attainment by all teachers interested in teaching high-achieving students. Ultimately, the general education program will benefit, and a three-year rotation can be developed. As the model continues over the course of several years and the need for additional cluster teachers increases, qualified teachers will become available.

Occasionally, the opposite problem exists, one in which no teacher wants to teach the high-achievers. In this case, the administrator should speak individually to each educator at that grade level to determine why no one is showing interest in the position. Often someone does really want to take on the challenge, but may not want to say so in front of the group. An interested teacher might feel afraid that colleagues will be jealous or that he or she is not qualified for the position. If this is the case, then the administrator can "appoint" the teacher to teach this class and allay any fears the teacher may have about the position. If, on the other hand, no one wants to teach these children, then it might be possible to reassign a teacher from another grade level. However, if teachers from other grade levels also feel the same way, then this administrator needs to do more work to create buy-in before attempting the model. Perhaps taking a year in which staff would read this book and other articles about the topic and take time for discussion and problem solving would encourage buy-in.

IMPLEMENTATION CONSIDERATIONS

As with any educational program, a model is only as strong as its theoretical underpinnings, research basis, and the people who implement it. This statement also holds true for Total Cluster Grouping. In order for this model to succeed, it requires knowledge of the students for whom the model is provided, a willingness to collaborate, and continuous professional development. In addition, the implemented model should reflect the community and cultures of the school in which it is developed.

Administrators

Strong administrative support is essential for effective implementation. The identification process alone will require time outside of class for teachers to identify and assign students to classrooms. With administrative support, this time can be made available. Administrators also play a key role in that this model affects the entire grade level and school. Without the leadership and support of the school's administrative team, from the school counselor to the principal, cluster grouping cannot be successfully implemented.

Administrators work closely with the public, and they should consider the role of parents in the support of this model. We suggest that parents be a part of the planning committee to help facilitate communication about and understanding of the model and how it will help teachers better meet the needs of students of all achievement levels. Some districts have developed a pamphlet that they send home to families (see Figure 2.3), others hold meetings, and still others answer parent questions as they arise. Administrators, working with their staff, can determine what will be most appropriate in the context of the school and community.

Data Collection and Evaluation

Districts that take the time, effort, and energy to implement a Total School Cluster Grouping Program should not do so without a plan to evaluate the effects and efficacy of the program. Most districts gather data on an annual basis. Evaluation need not be an additional burden; it can be a planned use of existing data and efforts.

What about other clusters besides high achieving?

By adopting the cluster model for elementary classroom assignment, the needs of all groups of students are taken into account.

Students in classrooms that do not have high achievers included will benefit because they will not be overshadowed, perhaps, by the high achieving students. In that way, other students can find that they, too, can achieve at higher levels.

The methods of addressing the needs of all students will be the same—differentiating of instruction and assessment in order to meet the needs of everyone.

Teachers will be able to differentiate more effectively with fewer skill levels in the same classroom, and all students will benefit.

This model maximizes learning for all students.

If I continue to have questions, where do I go?

The building principal of the school your child attends is in the best position to answer any questions you might have.

Converse Elementary:	Valree Kinch, Principal 395-
Sweetser Elementary:	Mike Keaffaber, Principal 384-
Swayzee Elementary:	Terry Renbarger, Principal 922-

Oak Hill United School Corporation

An Explanation of the Total School Cluster Grouping Model to Determine Classroom Assignment

Outside pages (1 and 4) of brochure

The Model

A group of parents, teachers, and administrators was formed in 2005 to study the issue of providing focused services for high achieving students.

As a result of that study and the assistance of professionals in the field, the "cluster grouping" model was selected as the preferred method of differentiating instruction and serving students at the elementary level in the Oak Hill United School Corporation.

Benefits of Total School Cluster Grouping

⇒ Research shows that cluster grouping improves student achievement among students from all achievement levels.
⇒ This model allows students with similar academic needs to work together during part of every day.
⇒ Clustering provides teachers with a structure for adjusting the curriculum and instruction to the achievement and skill level of the child.
⇒ This tool allows teachers to serve all students effectively and differentiate instruction to meet the needs of all students.
⇒ This model maximizes learning for all students.

How are students placed in a cluster?

All students are identified for small group instruction in a cluster group. Results from several grade level appropriate assessments such as NWEA, ISTEP+, DIBELS, STAR Reading, STAR Math, and teacher recommendations all play a role in this determination, as well as the special needs of individual students.

Will students stay in the same cluster throughout their elementary experience?

While cluster groups are generally stable, the assessment of students is an ongoing part of providing the best educational experience. These groups are flexible enough to allow changes as needed to better meet the needs of the student. Re-evaluation of all students is done annually.

How will instruction be differentiated for students who have demonstrated that they are ready to handle much more challenging work?

Most students at a particular grade level fall within a fairly narrow range around what most professionals would define as grade-level skills. This will vary with the content area, the skill, and the student. Some students enter a grade level already having mastered many of the skills typically taught at that grade level. Those high-achieving students need additional challenge.

Instruction for students in the high-achieving cluster in grades one and two will focus primarily on mathematics and literacy development. In grades three through five, students will have more opportunities to integrate and apply skills in the content areas of science and social studies as well. In grade six, expectations for students in this cluster will be defined for the content areas of mathematics, science, reading, writing, and social studies.

An annual plan for mathematics instruction for this group of learners will be determined through the use of a thorough pre-assessment of skills already mastered. Once the grade level skills yet to be mastered have been identified, students will move through this work at a faster pace. They will then study skills that are outlined in the Indiana Standards for the next grade level, using above grade level materials. In addition, students will be challenged to solve more complex, difficult problems and will be pushed to develop higher level thinking skills. These students will progress through above-level materials as time allows, but will not necessarily be expected to master all of the standards at the next grade level.

In the areas of language arts, science, and social studies, additional challenge will be provided through project selection, the choices and options offered to the students, and the materials used for instruction. These students will also be expected to read and discuss more advanced literature. Curriculum for this group will be extended to develop the depth of understanding of a topic or theme in keeping with the students' strengths and capabilities.

Inside pages (2 and 3) of brochure

Figure 2.3. Brochure for parents explaining the Total School Cluster Grouping Model. Used with permission.

To fully understand the program's effects on all students, data from all students, not just those identified as high achieving, must be examined. We recommend maintaining records of identification categories over time to help understand if the program results in more students being identified as achieving at higher levels and fewer students being identified at lower levels. This task is as simple as setting up a spreadsheet workbook containing students and their identification categories over time, or adding a column to the district database on each student if such a database exists. Identification data coupled with individual student achievement scores can provide an informative picture of how the program functions. Comparing these data with baseline data or data from a school in the district not using cluster grouping can provide more insights into the actual effects of total school cluster grouping. Identification data and achievement data examined together with classroom practices and school climate data can provide a comprehensive program evaluation from which adjustments and improvements can be made.

Meeting with staff to discuss what works and what needs to be improved can also result in program improvements. For example, in our study school, teachers suggested clustering the learning-disabled students and team-teaching them. This suggestion resulted in an effective addition to the program that allowed colleagues to work together to address the special needs of these students.

Underrepresented Populations

Another important consideration involves whether the students identified as high-achieving proportionally represent the demographic student population of the district and school in which the program exists. The field of gifted education is plagued by the under-identification of children from certain minority groups (i.e., African American, Latino/a, Native American) and of children living in poverty (Gentry, Hu, & Thomas, 2008). In this model, such under-identification is easily dealt with as no limits are placed on how many children can be "identified." In other more exclusive models with limits on the number of seats in the gifted program, identifying a child from poverty who has potential might result in services denied to another child who already achieves at high levels. In the Total School Cluster Grouping Model, both of these children can be identified and receive services. An examination of who is identified as high achieving at the beginning of program development (as a baseline) will provide valuable information concerning the equity of access to programming efforts. Over time, as they develop skills and confidence, more children should be identified as high achieving. The proportion of children identified as high achieving from diverse cultural backgrounds and from poor socio-economic backgrounds should be a part of the increase and mirror the population of the school as a whole. If the program does not develop in this manner, then school personnel should intervene, include in the high-achieving clusters children who show potential, and provide children from underrepresented populations with the extra support they need to reach their individual potentials.

REACHING OUT TO PARENTS

In our work with this program during the past two decades, we have found that educators are often worried about how to explain this model to parents. First, let us say that concerned parents are an asset and not a liability. Often the questions parents ask serve to increase accountability and educational quality. Parents can become strong advocates for effective programs like Total School Cluster Grouping if they are provided with information about the program. Thus, developing brochures and presentations that explain the program to parents (as shown in Figure 2.3 on page 32) is a very good idea.

We have found in our work that the best approach in dealing with parents is one of open communication. First, parents often want to understand how (and why) students are identified for placement in particular classrooms. School personnel should start by explaining that *all* classroom teachers differentiate curriculum and instruction, and that the Total School Cluster Grouping Model enables *all* teachers to better address the educational and affective needs of *all* their students. Program leaders can go over the achievement categories with parents just as they do with teachers, but without the educational jargon. Stress that the categories

- are not fixed,
- are used for placement purposes,
- reflect the child's achievement in school at that time relative to others in the same grade, and
- are a combination of observed performance and achievement measures that are used to include, not exclude, students in achievement groups.

Next, they can explain that students will be grouped for instruction based on skill levels in reading and math to promote optimal learning and growth. If the school supports regrouping among classes within the grade, parents will want to know about that practice as well. Program leaders should describe how all classrooms will contain students who achieve at above-average levels and explain how this arrangement as well as regrouping by skill level promotes academic growth for all levels of students. School personnel should ensure that parents understand that students will be re-identified each year and that the number of students who can be identified at high-achieving levels is not limited. In addition, many parents like to hear about accountability; therefore, program leaders should be sure to stress the research findings on the model and the school's plan for tracking program effects.

Second, sometimes issues arise when parents request that their child be placed in a particular classroom. This request presents a problem only when the student for whom the placement is requested achieves at an above-average level and the parents are requesting that he or she be placed in the high-achieving cluster classroom. In this model, it is important to place above-average achieving students into other classrooms (not the high-achieving cluster classroom). When such requests occur, we suggest that school personnel explain to parents how their son or daughter's achievement level compares with other students who will be in the cluster of high-achieving students. Even though their child has been identified as above average, he or she will likely fall among the bottom of the high-achievers. A year of being in another classroom among his or her academic peers may contribute to academic growth and boost academic self-confidence. In fact, the child may be among the top students in the class. School personnel can remind parents that differentiation will occur in *every* classroom and *all* students will be challenged. In addition, students will be re-identified each year for appropriate placement. Finally, if the parent is not satisfied, school personnel can schedule another meeting after six weeks to assess whether the student is thriving in his or her placement. We have found that after approximately six weeks, most students (and thus most parents) are happy with their classroom experience. But, if after six weeks the placement does not appear to appropriately address the child's needs, then a move should be considered.

Third, issues can arise when parents perceive that all of the quality educational experiences occur in the classroom with the cluster of high-achieving students. For a successful implementation of this model, all classrooms must offer students appropriately challenging and engaging learning experiences and proudly display the results of those experiences. All classroom teachers should employ differentia-tion strategies and engage in gifted-education pedagogy. All classroom teachers must have high expectations of their students. A trip down the hall in an effectively cluster-grouped school should reveal few differences among classrooms to the casual observer. In other words, all classrooms should be enriched, and all students should be engaged in projects and learning experiences that address their interests and talents. Such engagement will help promote achievement among all students in the school. (These strategies are addressed in Part II of this book.)

Finally, once students are in the cluster-grouped classrooms, sometimes parents raise concerns about the work being too hard or their children experiencing frustration. This initial bump in the road is a normal occurrence. Teachers should emphasize that it presents an opportunity for students to learn to work hard and rise to meet challenging curriculum. It is much better for students to be challenged and receive marks below 100% than for them to move through school obtaining great grades with little effort (Robinson, Reis, Neihart, & Moon, 2002).

The identification and placement of students is an important and time-consuming task. Likewise, assigning teachers to classes is vitally important to program success and buy-in. However, it is what takes place after placing students and assigning teachers to particular classrooms that really makes the model successful. In Chapter 3 we address all aspects of professional development from initial training to on-going and in-depth support. We also discuss classroom practices, the use of grouping, and the role of teachers in the Total School Cluster Grouping Model. In Chapter 4 we discuss how the Total School Cluster Grouping Model fits with other gifted and school-based initiatives.

3

PROFESSIONAL DEVELOPMENT & CLASSROOM PRACTICES

Prior to implementation it is important that the team of school personnel makes a commitment to professional development. Within each classroom, teachers will be dealing with a narrower range of students, but students will still present a variety of needs. Therefore, professional development focusing on grouping, differentiation, and meeting the needs of high-ability learners will be required for the entire staff. Initially, the school personnel may need to seek help from professional consultants to conduct such training. As the program develops and teachers become more comfortable and well-versed in strategies that work, the need for outside presenters will lessen. However, there is always merit in keeping perspective by including strategies and ideas from professionals outside of your local program. Good professional development is perpetual and needs-based. Even the best models and strategies continually need to be revisited and updated to fit the needs of a school's current population.

In addition to understanding how to identify and place students in the model, a thoughtful and comprehensive staff development plan can lend needed support to enhance the success of the model. The importance of this plan cannot be overemphasized. One only has to look at the "mission statements" posted in nearly every school across the country and compare them to the practices that run contrary to these stated missions to realize that without planning, dialogue, and buy-in, program changes are not likely to matter (Fullan, 2006; Senge, 1991).

Professional development is so integral to the success of any program that it must be carefully considered from the beginning phases of implementation through advanced program development and refinement. Gentry & Keilty (2004) investigated the implementation of professional development associated with two different applications of cluster grouping—from program start-up to program maintenance. Key findings included the importance of initial discussions to develop vision and buy-in among staff. These discussions were followed by initial staff development on the how and why of the program and the details about how to implement identification and set up the classrooms. In this phase of staff development, research and effective practices became an important underpinning of program development. At the research implementation site, staff development initiatives often originated from teachers' requests or questions. In other words, once the program begins, asking teachers what they need in terms of professional development can be a responsive method of helping ensure their success.

We recommend that all gifted education staff development be open to all teachers, whether or not they are directly responsible for high-achieving students. In our study, we found that all teachers had participated in some staff development concerning gifted child education and all teachers used some gifted education strategies in their classrooms, reflecting what Ward (1981, p. 76) termed "a radiation of excellence."

In this study, we also found that a teacher who was an expert in gifted child education was also serving as a resource for other teachers in the building (Gentry & Keilty, 2004). Several teachers in our study explained how valuable the staff development in gifted education had been for them, and how, when they had questions about what to do with their high-achieving students, they simply asked their knowledgeable colleague in the building. Finally, we recommended several steps to maintain and develop the program including evaluation, research, and reflective practices that consider the achievement and growth of all students in the school.

Because the Total School Cluster Grouping Model fits seamlessly with the work of Renzulli and Reis, all teachers involved in the cluster grouping study were provided with a general overview of gifted education and talent development based on the three-ring conception of giftedness (Renzulli, 1978) and the Enrichment Triad Model (Renzulli, 1977; Renzulli & Reis, 1997). The three-ring conception of giftedness views giftedness as a behavior that results from the interaction of three traits: above-average ability, task commitment, and creativity. When the three traits interact and are brought to bear upon a specific human endeavor, gifted behavior occurs. Renzulli believes that gifted behaviors can be developed in students who are given appropriate opportunities to develop their strengths and interests. He proposed the Enrichment Triad Model as a means for developing talent in more students.

In this model, three types of enrichment activities are provided for students, and there is an interaction among these types of enrichment, with each leading to and reinforcing the others. Type I Enrichment comprises exploratory activities designed to expose students to a variety of topics and areas of study not ordinarily covered in the regular curriculum. Type II Enrichment consists of group training in thinking and feeling processes, learning-how-to-learn skills, research and reference skills, and written, oral, and visual communication skills. Type III Enrichment engages students in first-hand investigations of real problems. The Enrichment Triad Model is based on ways in which people learn in a natural environment, rather than the artificially structured environment that characterizes most classrooms. Using the Enrichment Triad Model activities was encouraged in all classrooms in our study sites. The wide implementation of gifted education strategies in all classrooms lessens the perception of a "gifted class" that engages in "better" learning activities. The climate becomes one of talent development in the school as a whole, with each class focusing on student strengths, talents, and interests.

CLASSROOM PRACTICES

Teachers in the cluster grouping study (Gentry, 1999) used a variety of strategies to meet the needs of individual students in their classrooms. Teachers who had clusters of high-achieving students used most of the strategies listed below. Most noteworthy, however, was that the other teachers also used these strategies. In this manner, the types of curriculum, instruction, and strategies that might most often be reserved just for students in a gifted program permeated the school in the cluster grouping study and likely led to the increase in student achievement. Specifically, in our study site, we found teachers

- integrating higher order thinking skills,
- developing critical thinking,
- teaching students to use creative thinking skills and think divergently,
- integrating problem solving,
- assigning long-term and high-level projects,
- using acceleration,
- adjusting assignments based on student skills,
- grouping students so they could spend time with like-ability peers,
- developing and implementing curricular extensions to challenge their students,
- providing students with choices of partners or groups,
- providing students with choices to work alone or together,

⚜ using open-ended questioning,

⚜ offering students independent study options,

⚜ using challenging questions,

⚜ implementing curriculum compacting (Reis, Burns, & Renzulli, 1992),

⚜ providing students with problem and assignment options,

⚜ providing enrichment experiences to students, and

⚜ having high expectations for student achievement.

These strategies are only as successful as the person implementing them. Not all teachers used all strategies, which underscores the fact that teachers are as different from each other as are their students. Any discussion concerning differentiation ought to include the notion of differentiation for teachers, as they differ from each other in their teaching methods, materials, and styles. For this reason, the above-listed strategies are intended to be a menu from which teachers might choose to improve their instructional repertoire. Total School Cluster Grouping demands that various activities take place in a classroom simultaneously. The role of the teacher expands to include facilitation, mediation, implementation, and inspiration. For the greatest successes with the students in these classrooms, there must be a positive environment and high, yet realistic, teacher expectations (Gentry, 1999). In other words:

> The cluster teachers plan activities of a progressively challenging nature. These learning activities may be considered "instead of" rather than "in addition to" the regular curriculum. We suggest to teachers that it can be interpreted as not "more of the same" but something "instead." For example, instead of answering a number of low-level comprehension questions at the end of a story, the student may be asked to describe the story's theme and analyze how it could apply to his/her own life. In another situation, cluster teachers may pretest their students on the content of the math unit to be covered during the next two weeks. Students who demonstrate mastery of that content on the pretest might then be directed towards an independent research study facilitated by a teacher. In some classrooms the teacher may design a lesson with sufficient depth and breadth to challenge all of his/her students. In some cases students might be accelerated through a portion of the curriculum. In other situations, teachers may decide to provide an enrichment unit that extends the learning into higher levels and newer horizons. These strategies may be used in any subject area with just the cluster students, a mixture

of cluster students and other students, or the whole class. The plans may be shared with other teachers. (Gentry & Keilty, 2004, p. 154)

THE USE OF GROUPING

The teachers in the study also used a variety of grouping strategies. The reason for grouping is to facilitate learning. Achievement grouping allows for teachers to adjust curricula based on the skill level of students, and other forms of grouping are equally effective tools for enhancing student learning. Teachers in our study used two forms of grouping in their efforts to help students achieve:

* Between-class groups, which included regrouping by achievement levels for reading and math four or five days per week. In this manner and for these two subjects, one teacher taught the advanced students, another teacher taught the struggling students, and the remaining teachers taught the average students using appropriately leveled materials that were high quality and interesting to the students at each level. The teacher who taught the students struggling with math or reading had help from a special education teacher-consultant and from a Title I aide.

* Within-class groups, which included grouping students by interest, in cooperative learning groups, as peer-learning dyads, and by achievement levels in subjects other than math and reading (as those subjects were addressed in the between class arrangements).

Key to both the within-class and between-class configurations of grouping was flexibility in the groups. As students gained in skills in the between-class arrangements, they were moved to higher skill groups, with some students being moved to higher grades. Whereas, a cluster-grouped classroom of high-achieving students might have had 10 students who excelled in both math and reading, the high-achieving reading section had 24 students who excelled in reading. The addition of 14 new students to the original 10 advanced readers created a new group of students with strengths in reading. By definition, this is a form of flexible grouping, which then provided advanced reading curriculum to able readers in a grade level. These procedures were also used for math instruction.

Regrouping for instruction facilitated the addition of students who excelled in math or reading to the core of high-achieving students who excelled in both subjects. Within the classes, grouping strategies used by the teachers were also flexible. Cooperative learning was used in both homogeneous and heterogeneous applications, and students in these classes worked with a variety of their classmates on a all types of schoolwork. Teachers also gave students the choice to opt out of group work if they would rather work alone.

When academically struggling students worked together in their achievement-grouped class in either math or reading, the teacher who instructed these groups used quality curriculum, had high expectations that these students would succeed, and presented the material at a pace and depth that facilitated student understanding. These students didn't have to worry about being behind or having other kids snicker if they asked a question because they didn't understand, and as a result, they began asking more questions. As they developed skills, they developed confidence, and as they developed confidence, they began to achieve. These instructional groups formed by grouping students of similar achievement levels in specific content areas served as an intervention for low-performing students. Similar students in other settings or schools might have remained low-performing and fallen further behind, but the students in this achievement-grouped setting began to make progress.

ROLE OF THE TEACHER

Realistically, any educational model is only as strong as the teachers who implement it. When teachers practice the following elements, cluster grouping can yield impressive results.

1. Foster and maintain a positive classroom environment.

Kids are observant beings. If teachers do not orchestrate a positive classroom environment from the start, students may recognize each other only for their different abilities instead of focusing on strengths and interests. When teachers work to adjust assignments, help students achieve success, and create classrooms where students want to be, positive results are probable (Gentry, 1999). Facilitating acceptance and understanding among classroom members creates a positive learning community in which risk taking is safe.

2. Maintain high, yet realistic expectations of all students.

Students perform based on the expectations of those around them. Teachers' expectations have profound influence on student performance. Therefore by maintaining high, yet realistic expectations students are more likely to reach their full potential. A focus on both long-term process and incremental success along the way not only helps to encourage students, but also provides them with an inherent sense of progress that is likely to stay with them beyond that specific classroom experience.

3. Implement strategies to challenge students and meet students' needs in the cluster-grouped classroom.

What is good for gifted students may also benefit other students. However, the reverse does not necessarily hold true. It is imperative that educators use foundational strategies that have proven successful in challenging gifted students. A wealth of research exists regarding strategies that work for this population and these strategies should be fully integrated within cluster grouping programs. Part II of this book deals in depth with appropriate and effective differentiation strategies.

4. Participate in ongoing professional development opportunities.

There is always more to be learned about good classroom practices and curricular development regardless of level of experience in education. Professional development can come in a variety of forms: from more formal inservice activities to regularly scheduled, focused conversations between colleagues. The regularity of such self-advancement is essential in meeting the needs of all of learners.

SPECIFIC SUGGESTIONS FOR STAFF DEVELOPMENT

First, the entire staff needs an introduction to the Total School Cluster Grouping Model. The companion CD to this book provides a short overview in a power-point presentation that is keyed to the content of this book. This presentation works well in staff meetings as a way to stimulate further exploration and staff discussion.

Sometimes it is necessary to hire a professional or to send a team to a workshop to develop deeper understanding of the model and generate more buy-in. Likewise, it is possible to develop the understanding and buy-in through engaging staff in reading, discussion, and planning. However, it is important to recognize that understanding the model and identifying and placing students in classes represents only the beginning step toward effective implementation.

We suggest that, at the very minimum, all staff receive introductory professional development about the Total School Cluster Grouping Model, characteristics and needs of high-ability students, curriculum compacting, differentiation, and the Enrichment Triad Model as a foundation for successfully implementing this model.

Beyond these introductory efforts, we recommend that administrators ask the staff what needs they have and then respond to their needs with targeted and on-going staff development. These efforts should include a variety of activities such as workshops, conferences, summer institutes, as well as bringing presenters and coaches to the school to assist faculty with their efforts in the classroom. Types of differentiation that can accompany the cluster grouping placements are discussed at length in Part II.

Effective implementation of the Total School Cluster Grouping Model involves a combination of professional development and effective teacher practices. Recognizing that implementing any model requires work, evaluation, and changes to create the best fit of the model into the specific school context will enhance the quality of the implementation. Involving the entire staff in the development and improvement of the program, as well as in the identification of areas for supportive staff development, will go a long way to creating buy-in and support. Finally, recognizing the benefits that this model has for all students and teachers will create a positive school climate and learning environment for all.

4

COMPLEMENTING OTHER SERVICES & PROGRAMS

THE CONTINUUM OF ELEMENTARY GIFTED EDUCATION AND ENRICHMENT SERVICES

Total School Cluster Grouping coordinates well with other school services including pull-out programs, the Enrichment Triad Model (Renzulli & Reis, 1994), the Purdue Three Stage Model (Moon, Kolloff, Robinson, Dixon & Feldhusen, in press), and even with self-contained programs or special school program options by offering another tier of services for students who may not initially qualify for the self-contained classroom. By offering a variety of services in the school to encourage the development of diverse talents among students, educators increase the likelihood of reaching and developing strengths among more students. Figure 4.1 on the following page contains a list of programs and services that can be implemented in elementary schools. Programs that tend to benefit all students are presented in bold text, whereas those that are traditionally designed for gifted and talented students remain in Roman.

As depicted in Figure 4.1, a rich variety of services exists to enrich the education of elementary students. General classroom enrichment should focus on that which is interesting to students and targets their strengths. Renzulli has suggested the addition of Type I experiences in classrooms to stimulate the interests of all students and the integration of Type II activities that help students develop and use their learning how to learn skills. Some teachers use thematic units to enrich their classrooms. In short, all classrooms in the cluster-grouped school should include enrichment. Discovery, inquiry, and problem-based learning are discussed in Chapters 7 and 8, and they add depth to the enrichment.

ELEMENTARY SCHOOL SERVICES

A well-designed program will include many options from this continuum at all grade levels. Services that are **good for all kids** are indicated in bold typeface. These options do not constitute a gifted program, but they do set the stage for discovery and development of talent in more children. *Adapted from work by Joseph Renzulli (1994).*

- **General classroom enrichment**
- **Discovery, inquiry, problem-based learning**
- **Enrichment clusters**
- **Differentiation**
- Curriculum compacting
- Individual and small group counseling
- Social, emotional, physical health
- Independent study in interest area
- Product/Service in interest area
- Total school cluster grouping, high-achieving cluster
- **Total school cluster grouping, all classes**
- **Between class grouping by skill level**
- Non-graded cluster grouping
- Within- and across-grade pull-out by targeted ability, subject and interest areas
- Self-contained classes, (single or multi-grade)
- Magnet schools
- **Career awareness**
- **Integrated technology**
- **Multicultural education**
- **Foreign language study**
- Individual options: internships, apprenticeships, mentorships, IEP, dual exceptionalities
- Acceleration options: Early admission, grade skipping, subject acceleration, dual enrollment in middle school classes
- Special talent programs: young writers' programs, Saturday and summer programs, Future Problem Solving Program International, Math Olympiad, Science Olympiad, math leagues, science fairs, talent searches, Odyssey of the Mind, Destination Imagination, Invention Convention, etc.

Figure 4.1. A continuum of elementary gifted education, enrichment, and acceleration services.

Enrichment Clusters (Renzulli, Gentry, & Reis, 2002), are a schoolwide application of the Enrichment Triad Model, designed to bring gifted education services to all students and teachers in the school, making them a good fit with the Total School Cluster Grouping Model. Educators using cluster grouping might want to consider adding an enrichment program to their school day, and can learn how to do so by consulting the book *Enrichment Clusters: A Practical Plan for Student-driven, Real-world Learning* (Renzulli, Gentry, & Reis, 2002).

Special programs for gifted, creative, and talented students provide enriched learning to students in specific areas of interest and are described at the end of Appendix B. These programs, with their extra-curricular feel, have the potential to elevate academics to the level of sports in the school. Science Olympiad medalists or Odyssey of the Mind team winners can be celebrated alongside the basketball, football, and track stars!

In our work, we found that "general" educators often borrowed from or used traditional gifted education materials, strategies, and approaches with their students. As one teacher put it:

> I've learned so much from [Teacher 3A] and I adapt many of the strategies that she uses with her high achievers and use them with my learning disabled and low achievers. I don't think that gifted education is just for gifted students. (Gentry & Owen, 1999, p. 238).

Thus, we encourage educators to view the continuum of services in the context of the distinct possibility that gifted education strategies and programs can benefit the general education program. We also encourage school personnel to consider offering many different options to students with a goal of reaching more students.

Pull-out, Push-in, and Send-out Programs

In any gifted program that requires a pull-out or send-out component, students who comprise a high-achieving cluster can be sent to the gifted resource teacher and only disrupt a few classrooms. Additionally, gifted education pull-out services are part-time, often as little as an hour a week. Total School Cluster Grouping offers full-time services to high-achieving students during the rest of their school experience, and thus complements pull-out services with intensive, regular services. This arrangement works equally well for any students who receive direct pull-out services for other special needs. For example, a cluster of English as a New Language (ENL) students may receive support services either as a pull-out or from a specialist who comes into the classroom. As a cluster, they can support each other; the teacher who has these students in her class can plan around their special services schedule, and a more consistent delivery of services can be maintained. Similar arrangements can be developed by clustering students who receive Title 1, Reading Recovery, Speech, and/or Special Education services in designated classrooms. A traditional pull-out application involves many teachers and classrooms, making it difficult to schedule and coordinate, and involving varying levels of support and buy-in from different classroom teachers. When the special needs students are pulled-out from a clustered classroom on a regular basis, fewer teachers are affected. The teacher of this classroom expects students to leave for services, supports the delivery of these services, and plans for instruction with the rest of the class during the pull-out time.

Similar to pull-out services are push-in services in which the specialist and education aides work in the classroom alongside classroom teachers. Total School Cluster Grouping facilitates push-in services by requiring that specialists and educational aides attend fewer classrooms. Thus, their time in the cluster-grouped classroom can be extended. In one of our study schools, each Title I aide spent five half-days per week in each of two classrooms. Similarly, in another school, the Teacher Consultant for students with Learning Disabilities was able to spend half days in fewer classrooms by working with students in cluster groups. In the push-in approach, students are not seen by other students as those who have to leave class. Moreover, the specialist or aide who works with these students becomes part of the classroom community, helping the targeted students, the classroom teacher, and often relating positively to other students in the classroom. Key to the success of this type of cluster is support for the classroom teacher from specialists and teaching aides who assist in addressing the targeted students' special needs.

Self-contained Classrooms and Magnet Schools

Some districts implement self-contained classes of gifted and talented students or send identified students to a magnet school setting. Such applications of gifted programming have merit and have been shown in the literature to benefit the gifted students whom they serve academically, socially, and emotionally (Delcourt, Loyd, Cornell, & Goldberg, 1994; Kulik, 2003). However, these programs have a downside—the limited number of students allowed into the program (Renzulli & Reis, 1997). This limitation also often precludes the addition of new students. If a district only offers a program in which a limited number of students can receive services in special classes or special schools, it runs the risk of missing those who could succeed in the program, such as students from impoverished backgrounds and students from cultural groups that continue to experience severe underrepresentation in gifted programs (Gentry, Hu, & Thomas, 2008; Miller, 2004; United States Department of Education, 2000). These programs also miss students who, after several years in school, catch up and develop into high-achieving students. Fortunately, programs do not have to be limited to a one-size-fits-all approach with only a limited number of options and spaces in the program.

Implementing Total School Cluster Grouping can work in conjunction with magnet schools and self-contained classrooms, thus extending services to more students, involving more teachers, and ultimately developing more talents among students. One might initially think that if students are being identified for a magnet school placement or for a self-contained class, then gifted students won't be available to be identified for placement in the high-achieving cluster classroom. However, we have not found this to be the case. On the contrary, selective magnet school or self-contained programs, due to their rigid identification protocols, often miss identifying high-achieving students who will then be identified in the cluster program. Further, parents sometimes decline to send their children "away" to the magnet program in order to keep them in the neighborhood school or with their friends, or due to fear of the program being too hard for their children. Total School Cluster Grouping offers these kids a safe placement in their home school. Moreover, it offers the opportunity to serve more students and to identify students additional students over time. Thus, this model complements existing magnet and self-contained programs that may be in place in a district. Our current study district includes a magnet school, and many very bright children attend each of the other (non-magnet) elementary schools that use Total School Cluster Grouping. These two services—magnet and cluster grouping—work well in this district. Total School Cluster Grouping offers districts yet another program on a continuum of services that complement each other in the development of student talents.

Departmentalization in the Upper Elementary Grades

Departmentalization involves grade-level teachers each focusing on a content area and students moving from teacher to teacher for content instruction. For example, one teacher might teach all of the science lessons, another all of the math lessons, and yet another all of the social studies lessons. In a departmentalized grade level, students have a homeroom and then move to the subject area teachers using a mutually agreed upon schedule. In the upper grades, departmentalizing is often done to add content expertise to the curriculum as well as to prepare students for middle school where changing courses and teachers is common practice.

Departmentalization can work with Total School Cluster Grouping; however, each content area teacher must agree to further differentiate for the section of students from the homeroom with the cluster of high-achieving students. Such agreement can enhance the reputation and quality of the grade-level teachers, as each of the grade-level teachers commits to learn and deliver curriculum to challenge identified high-achieving cluster students. Thus, all teachers develop skills in working with advanced students and create curriculum and curricular extensions to meet these students' needs. These skills can ultimately result in increased expertise and enriched curriculum that benefits all learners at the grade level.

Sometimes, by the time students reach the upper elementary grades, a classroom of high-achievers exists. In such a case, teachers in a departmentalized arrangement would have one of their classes comprised of advanced learners. Unfortunately, this arrangement prevents moving students with strengths in only one academic area in and out of clusters as previously discussed unless the grade-level team invents some creative scheduling to accommodate individual students.

Multi-age Programs

Applying Total School Cluster Grouping to multi-age or looped settings needs further study. However, in each of these settings common sense in conjunction with the goals of this model should dictate practice. In a multi-age setting, high achievers from each grade level should form the cluster, and students of other achievement levels should be placed as recommended in Chapter 2. In a looped classroom, one in which the teacher moves up a grade level with her classroom, it might be necessary to add new students during the second year of the loop. This case is especially true if the teacher who loops also teaches the high-achieving group of students. If more students are identified as high achieving each year, then these students may need to be placed in her classroom in the second year of her loop. If two clusters of high-achieving students are formed, then this arrangement may not be necessary.

The Enrichment Triad Model and The Purdue Three Stage Model

The Enrichment Triad Model (Renzulli & Reis, 1994) involves a component in which students revolve into the program for in-depth pursuit of Type III investigations and for intensive training in methodological skills. While this model employs a revolving door and can involve a variety of students, those students who have been identified as high-achieving in the Total School Cluster Grouping Model will likely require services in the Enrichment Triad Model. Further, as discussed in Chapter 3, the Enrichment Triad Model can serve as the basis for Schoolwide Enrichment and for extending gifted services to students in all classrooms.

Such is the case in the Purdue Three Stage Model (Moon, Kolloff, Robinson, Dixon & Feldhusen, in press), in which gifted and talented students pursue advanced academics by moving through three stages of more intense study with a final project as an outcome. Stages I and II focus on providing content knowledge and enhancing problem-solving skills. Stage III involves self-directed inquiry and the development of a product for an audience, much like Renzulli's Type III, but focused more closely on an academic area of study. Both of these programs involve a pull-out component that would assist the teachers of the high-achieving cluster students with delivery of advanced services to their students as well as provide these teachers with time to work with the other students in small groups in their classrooms.

Finally, when considering implementing cluster-grouping and how it can work with existing or potential services, district personnel should note how this total school model can supplement their existing efforts and bring services to more students, schools, and teachers. Implementing the Total School Cluster Grouping Model should never be used as rationale to eliminate other viable services available or potentially available to students. It is only through a continuum of special services that student talents can be developed effectively. Total School Cluster Grouping offers districts a method of placing students in classrooms in a manner that can help teachers better meet their academic needs and help all of their students achieve at higher levels. Total School Cluster Grouping done in conjunction with other services simply makes sense.

By grouping students in clusters, classrooms are organized to meet the student's individual needs. The strategies teachers use to challenge and meet their students' needs are integral for student growth and true model implementation. These strategies and supporting resources are the focus of Part II of this book.

PART II

5

WHAT IS DIFFERENTIATION?

Going through the effort of identifying achievement levels and carefully assigning students and teachers to particular groups is the first step in raising achievement in the Total School Cluster Grouping Model. But in our studies we found that it is the type of teaching made possible by cluster grouping that resulted in increased achievement scores. These teachers were involved in enrichment teaching and learning (Renzulli & Reis, 1997). They did not make a concerted effort to increase their students' test scores due to external accountability pressures—a theme all too common in today's schools. Instead, we believe that the *enriched teaching* led to increases in student achievement. We caution school personnel to resist the urge to provide only high-achieving students with enriched curricula and advanced content and focus primarily on the deficits (as identified by test scores) of the rest of the students. We urge educators to develop all cluster-grouped classrooms into learning environments that engage students in challenging, meaningful, appealing curriculum and instruction targeted toward their strengths, interests, and talents. In this atmosphere, cognitive growth will occur, motivation will increase, self-efficacy will be enhanced, and higher achievement will follow.

The key to achievement in all students is the use of differentiation in the classroom. This idea is not new; think of the teacher in charge of a one-room schoolhouse who worked to serve students of varying ages and abilities. He or she understood the readiness levels of his or her students and accommodated the inevitable differences that occurred when 6 and 16-year-olds learn in the same classroom. Although individualized instruction was typical in the one-room schoolhouse, in today's differentiated classroom, teachers generally limit the options to several different learning experiences, and these are often based on student choice (Tomlinson, 1999).

Differentiated instruction draws from best practices in gifted education and has evolved over the years in response to extensive research on learning and brain functioning, as well as gifted education pedagogy (Roberts & Inman, 2007; Wormeli, 2006). Differentiated instruction maximizes student growth by responding to student learning profiles and interests. Teachers recognize student commonalities and differences and create tasks that vary by difficulty and match students' achievement levels. Differentiation in the classroom provides all students with the opportunity to engage in meaningful learning experiences that are appropriately challenging.

The current focus on testing has resulted in an over-emphasis on skills-based instruction (Amrein & Berliner, 2002; Gentry, 2006). Skills-based instruction need not be limited to a direct teaching approach. The curriculum is *what* educators teach—the skills and knowledge teachers expect students to gain during their time in school. It is essential to understand *the what* in order to determine *the how*. Differentiated instruction is *how* educators teach—the strategies and techniques used to ensure that students acquire necessary skills and knowledge while participating in engaging and challenging activities that address their readiness level. Differentiated instruction allows teachers to easily embed challenge, choice, and meaningfulness into lessons while increasing appeal and self-efficacy, factors that increase motivation and form the basis for many curricular and instructional differentiation efforts (Renzulli, Leppien, & Hays, 2000; Tomlinson, 1995, 1999).

Gentry and colleagues suggest that constructs of appeal, challenge, choice, meaningfulness, and self-efficacy influence and guide teachers' differentiation efforts (Gentry & Gable, 2001; Gentry & Owen, 2004). By consistently incorporating these constructs into their planning and instructional efforts, teachers can develop an effective differentiated learning environment.

Appeal

According to Gentry & Owen (2004), *appeal* combines elements of interest and enjoyment. Learning should and can be an enjoyable experience. Enjoyment, thinking, and attention increase as interest in the topic increases: "Learning is more effective when students enjoy what they are doing, and, therefore, learning experiences should be constructed and assessed with as much concern for enjoyment as for other goals" (Renzulli, 1994, p. 204). Determining student interests and planning differentiated activities that parallel those interests will result in effective lessons that appeal to the students and consequently lead to higher achievement.

Challenge

Learning occurs best when instruction appropriately challenges children by targeting their Zone of Proximal Development (ZPD) (Vygotsky, 1978). The ZPD is the range that spans what an individual can do on his or her own and what he or she is not able to do independently. It is the level of instruction that appropriately challenges the student, yet does not frustrate him or her, where the possibility of success is neither too high nor too low. The ZPD is dynamic and constantly changes as the student acquires new knowledge and skills. It also varies widely from student to student: what one student finds challenging another student may find easy. Cluster grouping assists teachers in providing appropriate challenges by reducing the range of achievement levels students present in each classroom.

Choice

Providing students with opportunities to make decisions about their learning environment or experiences is highly motivating. As Csikszentmihalyi and his colleagues have said, "A measure of choice is arguably the ingredient most crucial to the realization of intrinsic rewards in the classroom" (Csikszentmihalyi, Rathunde, & Whalen, 1993, p. 186). The vast majority of schools in America include the phrase "develop life-long learners" in their mission statements. Students who take charge of their learning at a young age develop the requisite skills needed to become such individuals. Life-long learners are motivated, and their motivation increases when they have the opportunity to make decisions and select learning activities (Bloom, 1985; Dewey, 1916; Renzulli, 2002). Strategies used when differentiating the curriculum empower students to make decisions about their learning. Throughout the school year, students should have opportunities to make choices about products, presentation styles, collaborators, content, and materials. By making these choices they become better problem solvers, develop a stronger interest in learning, and enjoy their educational experiences.

Meaningfulness

For learning to be optimal, the content must be interesting, relevant, and meaningful (Phenix, 1964). Think about the times when learning was exciting. Chances are it was because the topic was enjoyable or there was a very good reason for learning it. Children are likely to learn much more about the environmental importance of wetlands if a developer decides to build a new shopping center on the empty lot next to a park where they had enjoyed listening to the sounds of nature coming from the neighboring peaceful marshland than they would from a class-room lecture. Connecting learning to a child's world and allowing the child to solve real problems that are relevant to the child increases the likelihood that he or she will achieve at high levels (Renzulli, 1982).

Self-efficacy

Self-efficacy relates directly to challenge. An individual's self efficacy reflects the person's confidence about his or her ability to perform a particular activity (Bandura, 1994). It would be natural to assume that Tiger Woods has high self-efficacy when it comes to playing golf. Most of us undoubtedly have much lower golf self-efficacy and would be thrilled to make it through a hole without loosing the ball multiple times. However, if we practiced golf for six hours a day, five days a week, for one month, our golf self-efficacy would increase. A person develops a sense of self-efficacy by exerting effort and successfully completing the task, whether physical or mental. Tiger has mastered golf; we have not. Practice will increase our self-efficacy more than Tiger's, as he already feels very efficacious about his golf ability.

Asking people to demonstrate skills they have already mastered does not increase their self-efficacy. Mairead spent the first five years of school listening to teachers exclaim about her incredible writing ability. The first drafts of her stories were consistently far superior to her peers' final drafts. In fifth grade, Mairead's parents decided that it was time for a creative writing mentor. For the first time in her life, Mairead was challenged to perform at a higher level. It was a difficult transition from always being the "perfect" writer to discovering that there was room for improvement. However, because she finally encountered a situation that required her to put forth effort, her self-efficacy about writing increased as did the quality of her stories.

Without challenge, self-efficacy does not develop and students settle into the belief that if they cannot do something quickly and with ease, then they must not be capable of doing it at all. Offering appropriate differentiated challenges based on individual needs is necessary for individuals to develop positive judgments about their ability to be successful.

THE DIFFERENTIATED CLASSROOM: GETTING STARTED

The differentiated classroom is a student-centered environment in which the students take ownership of their learning. Therefore, the role of the teacher is redefined. Instead of being the "sage on the stage" the teacher becomes the "guide on the side." Teachers in differentiated classrooms facilitate student learning as students participate in work that is challenging, meaningful, interesting, and engaging. Flexibility and openness to change are key characteristics of teachers who effectively create differentiated classrooms (Tomlinson, 1999). They are able to alter instruction in response to student needs and manage instructional time in a way that not only meets the standards, but also provides challenge and motivates students. To effectively use differentiation in the elementary classroom, it is essential that teachers

* know their students' strengths and interests,
* know what they want their students to understand,
* treat assessment as an ongoing diagnostic activity that guides instruction, and
* have a repertoire of teaching strategies and instructional activities.

Although achievement levels are used to place students in clustered classrooms, not all children in each cluster will come to class with the same background knowledge and skill-level in all areas. A teacher cannot assume that because a group of children have all been identified as high-achieving, they will all have the same prerequisite knowledge in all subject areas. Conversely, all students identified as low-average achieving do not necessarily need remediation in all areas. Also, an average-achieving student will not necessarily have his or her needs met if he or she is automatically placed in "on grade level" activities for every assignment. Hence understanding students' strengths, interests, skill levels, and knowledge bases leads to more effective student-centered instruction.

Curriculum can be differentiated by content, process, and product (Kaplan, in press; Kaplan & Cannon, 2001; Tomlinson, 2001) and can include different types of audience (Renzulli & Reis, 1997). Following is an explanation of each area.

Content

Content, what students study, can be differentiated for students who have already mastered the skills and knowledge to be taught or for students who quickly grasp concepts. Likewise, content can be modified for students who learn at a slower pace, or who struggle with certain topics. Differentiating content involves putting more depth into the curriculum through acceleration and high-level enrichment activities for the advanced learners and creating interesting and reinforcing lessons and activities for those who require more time to achieve mastery. The goal of content differentiation is to remove the learning ceiling and thereby allow students to move through the material at a pace that provides for continual intellectual stimulation. Teachers can modify content by altering the complexity and abstractness of concepts. High-achieving students can focus on relationships and generalizations rather than concentrating on facts and descriptions. They may work through the material at an accelerated pace or investigate novel and sophisticated ideas. They may also explore content not typically studied at their current grade level. Teachers should vary the content in response to student achievement.

Process

Teachers can vary *process*, how students learn what they learn, by using diverse instructional strategies, providing different materials for students, and offering different levels of support or scaffolding for open-ended activities. Students process information differently depending on their learning profile, interest, and prior knowledge. First-grade students who are not yet reading will not be able to process new information if given a third-grade textbook to read; yet, a first-grade student who taught himself to read at the age of three might significantly increase his understanding of a concept using the third-grade text. The objective is to encourage students to develop creative and critical thinking skills while they acquire new knowledge.

Stage II of the Purdue Three Stage Model (PTSM) (Moon, Kolloff, Robinson, Dixon & Feldhusen, in press) and Type II activities of the Enrichment Triad Model (Renzulli, 1977; Renzulli & Reis, 1997) are examples of methods for encouraging process differentiation. PTSM Stage II activities enhance students' complex problem-solving skills through the use of shared inquiry, creative problem solving, problem-based learning, discovery learning, and design tasks (Moon et al., in press). Type II activities promote the development of thinking and feeling processes, including creative problem solving, critical thinking, problem solving, communication skills, and advanced methodological skills in an interest area (Renzulli, 1977; Renzulli & Reis, 1997). The methods and strategies used in both of these models provide students with opportunities to engage in higher levels of thinking regardless of their current achievement levels.

Product

How students express their understandings or demonstrate what they have learned—in other words, *product*—can be tailored to student readiness, interest, or learning profile. Educators frequently use tests to assess student understanding of concepts. At times teachers allow students to select from a menu of possible products, thereby allowing students to work in their area of strength or interest. A child who excels in art may choose to create a diorama, while a child with verbal strengths may opt to write a play.

A problem with giving students a choice of products is that it does not guarantee that they will be challenged or have the opportunity to show what they have learned. High-quality product development occurs when students demonstrate recently acquired knowledge and skills. Creating the product should be a learning experience not just an opportunity to perform. Teachers must be conscious of the sophistication of the product as "The product assignment should stretch students in application of understanding and skill as well as in pursuit of quality." (Tomlinson, 2001, p. 86). The product should be focused on real problems and address authentic audiences rather than be an avenue for simply reciting information. The Products Planning Guide (Renzulli, Gentry, & Reis, 2003) lists a range of possible products in seven areas of product development: Artistic, Performance, Spoken, Visual, Constructed, Leadership, and Written Products. An abbreviated version appears in Figure 5.1 (with the full guide in Appendix A). Teachers and students have used this guide to help them think of alternative and creative ways to share knowledge.

Audience

Audience refers to those who have a vested interested in the student's product. When students explore content and process within the context of a real-world problem with the potential to affect a real audience, student learning is more meaningful and enjoyable (Renzulli, 1994). Providing the opportunity to develop an authentic product for a real audience motivates students to find effective ways to communicate and improve the quality of the product (Kettle, Rizza, & Renzulli, 1998). For a group of students who researched the lack of synchronization of the clocks in their school building, the audience might be their head custodian. The town council could be an audience for students studying local wetlands and the effect of their possible elimination due to a proposed development. When students realize that their work has the potential to make a difference, learning and performance escalate. When striving for authentic learning, content and process should be driven by the product, which is shaped by the audience.

Type III activities in the Enrichment Triad Model (Renzulli, 1977; Renzulli & Reis, 1997) result in the ultimate culmination of content, process, product, and audience and provide authentic assessment of learning goals with meaning beyond the classroom. These activities are born from student interest and provide opportunities for students to assume the role of first-hand inquirers. The outcome is an authentic product affects on a specific audience. Through participation in these activities and creation of authentic products, students learn organizational skills, gain content

Table 5.1. Abbreviated List of Possible Student Products.

Artistic Products			
Architecture	Batik	Landscaping	Puzzles
Murals	Exhibits	Terrariums	Car designs
Decoration	Cartoons	Mosaic	Maps
Sculpture	Book covers/designs	Collage	Sewing

Performance Products			
Skits	Dance	Films/videos	Interpretive song
Role playing	Mime	Reader's theater	Composition
Simulations	Puppet shows	Poetry readings	Chorale
Theatrical performance	Dramatic monologues	Improvisations	Concerts

Spoken Products			
Debates	Lecture	D. J. shows	Book talks
Speeches	Mock trials	Panel discussions	Chronicles
Radio plays	Songs	Celebrity roasts	Forums
Advertisements	Sales promotions	Narrations	Sign language

Visual Products			
Videos	Layouts	Ice sculptures	Maps
Slide/digital photo shows	Models	Demonstrations	Diagrams
Computer printouts	Pottery	Cartoons	Mobiles
Sculptures	Proclamations	Travel brochures	Set design

Models/Construction Products			
Drama sets	Gardens	Bird houses	Instruments
Sculpture	Dioramas	Bulletin boards	Robots
Relief map	Shelters	Circuit boards	Machines
Habitat	Collections	Paper engineering	Rockets

Leadership Products			
Speeches	Mock trails	Open forums	Service learning projects
Plans	Musical performances	Fund raising	Editing a newspaper
School patrols	Elections	Student council/government	Directing a plan
Leading rallies	Debates	Organizing a business	Discussion group on Internet

Written Products			
Pamphlets	Parables	Analyses	Budgets
Brochures	Advertisements	Epics	Criteria listings
Books	Laws	Web pages	Census reports
Speeches	Graphs	Autobiographies	Folktales

Adapted from Renzulli, J. S., Leppien, J. H., & Hays, T. S. (2000). *The Multiple Menu Model*. Mansfield Center, CT: Creative Learning Press.

knowledge, and develop a sense of self-efficacy (Renzulli, 1977; Renzulli & Reis, 1997). Type III activities naturally differentiate instruction because of the emphasis on student interest, authentic process, relevant products, authentic audience, and the activities' open-ended format.

The ultimate goal of differentiated instruction is to provide a learning environment that is academically responsive to individual student's needs to maximize student achievement and success.

KNOW YOUR EDUCATIONAL GOALS

Sometimes educators teach a unit or concept without a strong grasp of the educational goals. Having an understanding of instructional goals provides a clear picture of the content and skills that students should learn. A solid understanding of what students should know is essential to differentiating the curriculum.

For example, the teachers on the fifth-grade team asked the enrichment teacher, Mr. Blake, to help them differentiate their unit on Native Americans. Mr. Blake asked, "What do you want your students to know?" In response, the teachers pulled out a series of activities and described them to Mr. Blake, "We have the students do this one first, and they like doing this activity, and then we do this one . . . " Mr. Blake again asked, "What do you want your students to know?" The fifth-grade teachers continued to show him the activities that comprised the current unit. Explaining the distinction between learning activities and learning goals, Mr. Blake asked, "What understandings, knowledge, and skills do you want your students to gain during this unit?" The members of the team realized that their focus had been on the learning activities and that they had not spent much time considering learning goals. After a lengthy conversation they concluded that they wanted their students to understand how life for the Native Americans in New England had changed from the days of colonization to present time. They also wanted students to compare and contrast their lives with the lives of Native American children in the 1600s. With learning goals in place, these fifth-grade teachers could now focus on how to differentiate the unit. The students became junior practicing professionals as they investigated topics that interest anthropologists: the food, shelter, clothing, language, folktales, legends, pottery, art, music, and symbols of Native Americans. They used the information they acquired about Native Americans to compare and contrast their lives with those of indigenous children of the 1600s. The students participated in a series of activities. Some of these lessons were ones the teachers originally showed Mr. Blake, but they now had a focus as they helped students deepen their understanding of the culture of the people who had lived on the land centuries before them.

KNOW YOUR STUDENTS

Most experienced teachers have looked forward to a particular classroom activity because of how well it has been received by students in prior years only to be surprised to find it a dismal failure with "this year's kids." Typically such a flop occurs when the teacher does not have a good grasp of the students' interests and understandings. Effective instruction and differentiation require knowledge of the student's strengths, learning profile, and interests. An excellent way to gain this knowledge is through the use of pre-assessment activities together with interest and learning profile inventories.

During the first week of school each year, Mr. Davis asked his third-grade students to complete Me, Myself, and I (Mann, n.d.) , one of many inventories available for use in the classroom (see Appendix A). Me, Myself, and I asks students to select their favorite subjects as well as their interest areas as they rank a variety of activity choices such as acting, arts and crafts, dance, community service, and science experiments. Learning profile questions are included and ask students to think about how they like to learn new material. Students also indicate how they like to share their knowledge by selecting from a list of options including acting, role playing, taking a test, explaining their reasoning, drawing a diagram, or creating a model. The inventory asks students to designate the type of environment in which they like to learn. In another section, students indicate whether they prefer to work alone, with an adult, or with peers. Students record outside of school activities as well as short and long term goals.

Mr. Davis used the information from the inventories to guide his planning throughout the year. Typically he involved his students in many collaborative and cooperative activities. One year, he noticed that a large percentage of his students preferred to work alone. Though he realized the importance of developing collaborative skills, he also respected his students' learning profile responses and made a conscious effort to plan activities that included group and individual work.

Interest inventories also allow teachers to incorporate student interests into lessons. As Mr. Davis developed a science activity related to simple machines, he decided to group his students based on interest. The students who were passionate about soccer used a soccer ball with their incline plane and lever. *NASCAR* enthusiasts were busy doing the same activity with model race cars, and the arts and crafts group used balls they had created with PlayDoh.

The Total Talent Portfolio (TTP) (Purcell & Renzulli, 1998) involves a data collection system designed to gather and record information and provide a comprehensive picture about each student's strengths, abilities, interests, and learning profiles. It provides a systematic method for recording and monitoring student information. The TTP is intended for use throughout a child's school career. New data are added annually, resulting in a comprehensive record of the student's talents, achievements, interests, and learning profiles.

The TTP distinguishes between two kinds of information: status and action information. Status information pertains to the student's natural aptitude and abilities, activities and topics of interest to the student, and instructional preferences including thinking and learning profiles. This is information already known about the students. Action information relates to accomplishments within normal classroom activities, student reaction to enrichment activities, and products created by the student both within and outside of the school environment. Action information reflects what has been recently learned about the student. By using status and action information, teachers can guide students toward activities that would be academically appropriate as well as enjoyable for them. As students mature, they can assume major responsibility for maintaining as well as determining what products and data should be included in the TTP.

The more teachers know about their students' strengths, learning profiles, and interests, the more effectively they can differentiate for these students. When a student exclaims, "I'm bored," or "I have nothing to do," the teacher and student can check an interest inventory or TTP and help the student overcome his or her boredom with a project or activity directly related to something the student finds interesting or important. Knowing the students provides teachers with the tools to share the responsibility for differentiation with the students in a manner that makes students partners in learning, rather than learners of lessons of which they may or may not have ownership.

Know Your Students' Knowledge and Skills: Pre-assessment

Pre-assessment informs classroom practice, a critical step in the differentiation process. This systematic method for gathering and using information about student readiness for the curriculum should be a regular feature in classrooms. Diagnostic pre-assessment allows educators to discover the academic readiness of specific students and should be used as a basis for making instructional decisions. It helps teachers avoid making assumptions about student readiness. Children with academic strengths need challenging curriculum, but it is a mistake to assume that just because they have been identified as high-achieving, they have mastered all of the grade-level curriculum. Conversely, it is also a mistake to assume that students who have not been identified for inclusion in the high-achieving cluster need to complete every lesson in every subject.

Mastery of content or skills can be confused with the ability to memorize and recall information quickly. Mastery of multiplication is not demonstrated by accurately solving 20 multiplication problems in one minute (Burns, 2000). A perfect multiplication timed-test only indicates that the student has the ability to memorize discrete information and quickly write answers. With a conceptual understanding of multiplication, a student is able to use a known fact to determine the answer of an unknown fact. For example, a student who has a conceptual understanding of multiplication may not be able to quickly recall the answer to 8 x 7, but may know that 8 x 5 = 40. He understands that since 7 − 5 = 2, he will need to add 2 more groups of 8 to the partial product of 40 in order to find the correct answer to 8 x 7.

$8 \times 5 = 40$ $\bullet\bullet\bullet\bullet\bullet\bullet\bullet\bullet$ $8 \times 7 = 56$ $\bullet\bullet\bullet\bullet\bullet\bullet\bullet\bullet$
$\bullet\bullet\bullet\bullet\bullet\bullet\bullet\bullet$ $\bullet\bullet\bullet\bullet\bullet\bullet\bullet\bullet$
$\bullet\bullet\bullet\bullet\bullet\bullet\bullet\bullet$ $\bullet\bullet\bullet\bullet\bullet\bullet\bullet\bullet$
$\bullet\bullet\bullet\bullet\bullet\bullet\bullet\bullet$ $\bullet\bullet\bullet\bullet\bullet\bullet\bullet\bullet$
$\bullet\bullet\bullet\bullet\bullet\bullet\bullet\bullet$ $\bullet\bullet\bullet\bullet\bullet\bullet\bullet\bullet$
$\bullet\bullet\bullet\bullet\bullet\bullet\bullet\bullet$
$\bullet\bullet\bullet\bullet\bullet\bullet\bullet\bullet$

Showing a visual representation of a mathematical concept or explaining the patterns that occur when exploring multiples demonstrates mastery, the memorization of facts does not.

As a teacher of a cluster of high-achieving fifth graders, Mrs. Kareet stated that she did not need to teach grammar to the group because, "They know it all already." The enrichment teacher asked her what pre-assessment she had used to make that determination. Mrs. Kareet stated that the students wrote beautifully, so they must know the grammar. After a brief discussion, the resource teacher convinced Mrs. Kareet to give the students the fifth grade language arts final exam as a pretest. The results revealed that all the students had mastered identifying parts of speech, four of the seven students correctly identified subjects and predicates, and none of the seven students correctly identified all of the prepositional phrases and subordinate clauses. Mrs. Kareet's assumption was incorrect. Just because her students used the language correctly did not mean they understood all of the standard English conventions. As a result of the pretest results, she was able to concentrate on teaching the high-achieving students phrases and clauses and fill in the gaps that the pretest revealed existed among these students.

Pre-assessment can take many forms in addition to the traditional book pretest that Mrs. Kareet administered. At the beginning of each new science unit Ms. Schlemann's students complete a five-minute "quick-write" that she uses as a pre-assessment. Her prompt to the students is, "When I say _____ (genetics, simple machines, volcanoes) what jumps into your brain?" It only takes Ms. Schlemann a few minutes to survey the quick-writes and identify the students who have extensive background knowledge of the topic, those who possess baseline knowledge, and the students for whom the topic is a new concept.

Table 5.1 contains a variety of pre-assessment options. Also included are statements teachers could use to introduce a pre-assessment activity to students. Mr. Herr found that the "Five Hardest" strategy works exceptionally well for his second-grade mathematics program. When the class is ready to tackle a new strategy, Mr.

Table 5.1. Pre-assessment Options.

Format	Teacher Comment
Student conference	I noticed you know quite a bit about _____. Tell me a little bit more.
K-N-W chart	In 3 columns list what you know, what you need to know, and what you want to know about _____.
Journal entry	In your journal tell me what you know about_____.
Make a list	List everything that comes to mind about _____.
Create a product	Use the data in the table and make a _____ (e.g. bar graph).
Mind map or concept map	Draw a mind map showing what you already know about _____ (genetics, communities, plants).
Textbook pretest	You will be taking a pretest today on _____ so that we can discover what you already know about this topic.
Five hardest	There are five problems on this sheet, you may or may not be able to find the answers. Make an effort to work through them, but it is OK if you are not able to figure out the answers.

Herr gives them five difficult problems. If students complete four of the five accurately and neatly, he knows that those students are ready to tackle more challenging material. While completing problems neatly is not a prerequisite for demonstrating knowledge of a topic, Mr. Herr discovered that by including neatness as a requirement, student scores increased as many of the errors due to sloppy handwriting were eliminated. And his students not only have the opportunity to demonstrate their knowledge, they learn effective test-taking strategies.

When administering pretests, teachers should explain to students the purpose of the pretest and emphasize that it is perfectly acceptable if they do not have knowledge of the topic. Students are about to be tested on material that they have not yet been taught, and educators should make sure that students understand that they are not expected to know any of the information. In doing so, teachers set the bar low and reduce the chances of frustration among the pretest-takers. Younger students, especially high-achieving students, are often under the impression that they should be able to do everything asked of them by their teacher. When confronted with an unfamiliar topic they may become stressed. Teachers can help relieve these students' anxiety by reassuring them that the assessment will provide information about what still needs to be taught. When students do not know everything, teachers are pleased to help them learn.

In summary, pre-assessment helps teachers identify the appropriate instructional level for the student and "ensure that struggling, advanced, and in-between students think and work harder than they meant to; achieve more than they thought they could; and come to believe that learning involves effort, risk, and personal triumph" (Tomlinson, 1999, p. 2). Pre-assessment should become a matter of consistent practice in the differentiated classroom. Results help to create a more streamlined approach to teaching and learning, reduce redundancies and boredom among students, and increase motivation to learn new material. In fact, in the cluster grouping study, we (Gentry & Owen, 1999) observed students who were not identified as high-achieving benefiting from pretesting in the same manner as the high-achieving students. They did not have to repeat material they already knew, and they quickly discovered that if they learned the content and demonstrated that learning on the pre-assessment, they would be allowed to move on to other, more interesting and challenging materials.

In this chapter we have discussed the foundation to the structure of a differentiated classroom. The ultimate goal of differentiated instruction is to provide a learning environment that is academically responsive to individual student's needs and that will maximize student achievement and success. A thorough understanding of student strengths, learning profiles, and interests as well as a keen awareness of learning goals must be in place before introducing the specific strategies described in Chapters 6, 7, and 8.

6

SPECIFIC DIFFERENTIATION STRATEGIES

Having determined learning goals, discovered students' interests, and assessed students' readiness, teachers are ready to plan and teach effective lessons. Different teachers will use different activities at different times and choose strategies and activities based on their individual teaching strengths and styles, as well as on their students' learning profiles, readiness levels, and interests. In this chapter we discuss three effective strategies for differentiating instruction: anchor activities, curriculum compacting, and tiered activities.

CURRICULUM COMPACTING

Curriculum compacting (Reis, Burns, & Renzulli, 1992) is a technique that allows a teacher to eliminate the repetition of mastered content and skills. Students who "already know it" or who can learn the material at an accelerated pace are allowed the opportunity to reduce or eliminate the amount of instructional time spent on the topic. Rather than sitting through lessons covering material that they have mastered, students participating in curriculum compacting are instead given the opportunity to investigate a topic of interest or specific, enriched content that typically is not covered in the grade-level curriculum.

The specific steps to the curriculum compacting process are as follows:

1. Know the essential content and skills the students should master.
2. Pre-assess students who may benefit from curriculum compacting and determine a level that indicates mastery (e.g., 80% to 90% accuracy).
3. Create a plan for any material the student needs to learn and excuse the student from lessons on mastered material.

4. Use student interests and strengths to determine replacement activities.
5. Keep a record of student progress.

An organizational tool, *The Compactor* (Reis, Burns, & Renzulli, 1992) (see Figure 6.1 and Appendix A) provides a mechanism for teachers to record learning goals, list the pre-assessment results, and keep track of the acceleration and/or enrichment activities. The Compactor not only helps teachers as they work with individuals or small groups of students, but it also helps teachers as they explain to parents their children's specific learning activities during the compacting process.

Small Group Curriculum Compacting

The first year that Mrs. Young used curriculum compacting in her classroom, she vowed she would never teach the "old way" again. She was impressed and surprised with the outcomes: continual learning for all students and fewer classroom discipline problems. Using pretesting benefited Mrs. Young's entire class, as the results of the pretest indicated that all but two students had mastered the first three lessons in the unit. Thus, Mrs. Young was able to eliminate three days of instruction by working independently with the two students who needed instruction in those concepts. The same students did not compact for every chapter. John and Arcelia

INDIVIDUAL EDUCATIONAL PROGRAMMING GUIDE
The Compactor

Prepared by: Joseph S. Renzulli
Linda M. Smith

NAME________ AGE____ TEACHER(S) ________ Individual Conference Dates And Persons Participating in Planning Of IEP

SCHOOL ________ GRADE____ PARENT(S) ________ ____ ____ ____ ____

CURRICULUM AREAS TO BE CONSIDERED FOR COMPACTING Provide a brief description of basic material to be covered during this marking period and the assessment information or evidence that suggests the need for compacting.	PROCEDURES FOR COMPACTING BASIC MATERIAL Describe activities that will be used to guarantee proficiency in basic curricular areas.	ACCELERATION AND/OR ENRICHMENT ACTIVITIES Describe activities that will be used to provide advanced level learning experiences in each area of the regular curriculum.

☐ Check here if additional information is recorded on the reverse side.

Figure 6.1. The Compactor (Reis, Burns, & Renzulli, 1992).

were compacted out of the math curriculum for every chapter, but other students in the classroom moved in and out of the compacted group, some frequently and some for only one chapter.

After a quick overview of each new math topic, Mrs. Young's students took a pretest on the content of the chapter. John, Kyle, Latisha, Arcelia, and Areem earned scores of 85% or higher indicating they had no need to sit through lessons designed to teach the content that they had already mastered. These five students, three of whom had been identified as high-achieving and two of whom simply achieved well in the math content area, worked on alternative math activities that Mrs. Young had assembled. Using a variety of resources, she developed a series of open-ended activities that challenged the students to think not just about the procedures used, but also the conceptual basis of mathematics. The majority of the activities did not have "one right answer," and she encouraged the students to work collaboratively on the problems.

John, Kyle, Latisha, Arcelia, and Areem's group worked independently on the advanced activities included in the packet while the remainder of the class worked on grade-level curriculum. Mrs. Young provided periodic encouragement and guidance to the compacting group. When the class began to learn how to measure angles, Kyle joined the lessons as his pretest results indicated that he did not understand angles or how to measure them. The students in Mrs. Young's class were familiar with flexible and fluid groupings and understood the need for different configurations, so Kyle's transition from one group to another went by relatively unnoticed. Occasionally, Mrs. Young would ask the entire compacted group to join the class for either an activity related to content that none of the students had mastered or a special activity.

Individual Student Curriculum Compacting

Michael had been devouring information on Ancient Egypt since he visited the King Tut exhibit the previous year. As Ms. Bridges, his teacher, began discussing the upcoming unit of study on Ancient Egypt, Michael thrust his hand into the air. He struggled to contain himself from blurting out every fact that came to his mind. After calling on Michael to answer a question, Ms. Bridges quickly realized that he undoubtedly knew more about Ancient Egypt than she did and that if she did not provide another option for him, he would not learn anything during the weeks to come. Pulling Michael aside at the end of class, she asked a few key questions to confirm her suspicions about the extent of his knowledge. She then explained to

Michael that it would not be fair for him to have to sit through the planned instruction, even though he did enjoy the topic, as she wanted him to learn something new. Ms. Bridges and Michael discussed a few other ancient cultures. Michael was quite knowledgeable about Ancient Greece, but knew little about Ancient China. Michael decided he would spend his time in class investigating Ancient China and his study would culminate with a presentation to his class on the similarities and differences between Ancient Egypt and Ancient China. Ms. Bridges asked Michael to think about what he would like to include on a learning contract for his studies. The next day Ms. Bridges and Michael finalized and signed the contract. Michael, who was not always the most diligent student, worked tirelessly over the next three weeks sometimes working in the classroom and often heading to the library. As the class wrapped up their study of Ancient Egypt, Michael shared his new knowledge with a multi-media presentation and a culminating Jeopardy challenge for the class.

Michael's teacher knew the essential content and skills that her students should master. Her pre-assessment of Michael was guided by this awareness as she quickly asked him a few key questions. Ms. Bridges was familiar with Michael's interests and strengths, as she had her students complete an interest inventory during the first few weeks of the school year.

During the time he was studying Ancient China, Michael took charge of his learning, and Ms. Bridges noticed that he was more attentive to his studies than he had been all year. He was working in an area of passion and was intellectually challenged by the higher level activities that he and Ms. Bridges had developed. It was his choice to study Ancient China, and the project had great appeal and meaning to him. Michael's work resulted in an increase in knowledge, a highly creative product, and heightened self-efficacy as he realized he could do more than he ever thought possible. For Michael, just as Csikszentmihalyi and his colleagues noted:

> Only when challenges and skills were felt to be high and working in tandem did all the varied components of well-being—cognitive, emotional, and motivational—come together for the students. Concentration was far above its normal classroom level, and self-esteem, potency, and involvement also reached their highest levels. (Csikszentmihalyi, Rathunde, & Whalen, 1993, p. 186)

Michael was not identified as a member of the high-achieving cluster group in his classroom. He was, however, highly motivated due to the fact that he was able to choose his area of study. This example underscores why the opportunity to participate in a curriculum compacting experience should not be limited to students who have been identified as high-achieving. In fact, in our cluster grouping study school, 11 of 14 teachers routinely used curriculum compacting, yet only three of these teachers had students in their classrooms identified as high-achieving (Gentry & Owen, 1999).

Mrs. Young used a standard textbook pretest to assess her math students. Ms. Bridges used a brief student-teacher conference to confirm what she observed during a classroom discussion. Both pre-assessments were appropriate in the given situations to confirm that the students had mastered the planned curriculum. By compacting the curriculum for these students, the teachers were able to proactively resolve classroom management concerns that evolve when students are not appropriately challenged. At the same time they were also able to provide engaging meaningful, appealing, and high-level activities for the students involved.

TIERED ACTIVITIES

In a differentiated classroom using tiered activities, all students are focused on the same content, essential understandings, and key skills. Tiered activities are parallel tasks that vary in complexity and depth with different levels of support or scaffolding and are developed in response to student readiness and performance levels. Activities can be tiered based on readiness, interest, or learning profile (Tomlinson, 2001). As this book is focused on the cluster-grouped classroom, the emphasis here will be on tiering by readiness. Properly developed tiered activities maximize learning and appropriately challenge students to work in their Zone of Proximal Development (Vygotsky, 1978).

Tiered activities are used to meet the needs of learners functioning at different achievement levels, yet exploring the same content. Teachers assign students a tier for a specific task based on achievement level or allow them to choose the activity they would like to do. At times students work in groups and at other times they work independently. Tiered activities frequently include three tiers: above grade level, at grade level, and below grade level. There is no required or even recommended number of tiers; the number should reflect the needs of the students in the classroom. Teachers may find that for one activity they need to develop three tiers to maximize learning for their students, and for another activity they might only create two tiers. However, over time, teachers will need to make adjustments in response to the students' needs. Following are the basic steps for developing a tiered activity:

1. Select the skill or key concept (the concept or skill is the same for all students).
2. Pre-assess and/or administer an interest inventory.
3. Develop an assignment that is challenging for the majority of the students.
4. Incorporate scaffolding strategies for students with fewer skills.
5. Adjust the activity to increase the depth, abstractness, and complexity for students with higher skills.
6. Assign students to the appropriate tier.

The importance of the first two steps was discussed in Chapter 5, and Step 3 (develop an assignment that is challenging for the majority of the students) should already be in place in the general curriculum and instruction. Steps 4 and 5 are what need to be developed. Scaffolding or support strategies to help students with fewer skills can vary widely and may include more direct questions, word banks, outlines, study guides, reading materials at the appropriate level, manipulatives, and step-by-step directions.

In preparation for a writing assignment on communities, Mr. Byers gave students who struggle to get their thoughts on paper a word bank to provide them with a wider range of vocabulary. When comparing and contrasting fairy tales from different cultures, he provided his novice readers with below-grade-level texts that were heavily illustrated. During a science activity designed to have the students identify recurring patterns in nature, Mr. Byers gave the students who needed more structure a list of categories to consider, such as weather, seasons, day, and night.

To increase depth, abstractness, and complexity for students with higher skills, teachers may ask them to use more difficult reading materials, glean information from primary source materials, use open-ended activities, view a situation from a different perspective, or use activities requiring them to evaluate, compare, and contrast. Mr. Byers' above-grade level readers used Junior Great Books texts (www.greatbooks.org), which had rich vocabulary and few illustrations. When considering recurring patterns in nature, the students who functioned well when engaged in open-ended activities were asked to brainstorm different patterns.

The activities described above are just a small sampling of the possible adjustments that teachers can make when developing tiered activities. Most tiered activities are teacher generated, but occasionally a student can develop or suggest an activity. Mrs. Stilwill's fourth-grade students had been studying famous people from their home state of Michigan. Their assignment was to write a biography of one of these prominent individuals in preparation for their Living History Museum. As they settled in to start writing, Marielle approached Mrs. Stilwill and asked, "Would it be okay if I wrote my biography of Henry Ford as a series of letters to a friend instead of as an essay?" Marielle's query was the birth of a tiered activity. Mrs. Stilwill not only told Marielle that she could write letters, but she also gave the option to all of her students. The majority of the students were content to write the biography as an essay, but three other students took on the challenge of writing from their public figure's point of view. The following year Mrs. Stilwill developed three tiers for her students and allowed them a choice of activity. Figure 6.2 below presents this tiered activity.

Tiered activities can be as simple as a single math problem and as elaborate as an entire unit. Math problems can often quickly be tiered by giving the high-achieving math students an answer and asking them for the problem as illustrated in the example in Figure 6.3.

There are times when it is appropriate to assign students to a tier. Other times it is best to allow students to choose the activity (tier) they would prefer. Another option for assigning activities is to recommend to students a "minimum" tier. An

---

Tiered Social Studies Activity: Biographies

Learning Goal: Students will take notes in a structured format to write a biographical summary. Students will understand that secondary source materials are developed by people who have researched events, but did not experience them directly.

Tier 1 These students benefit from structure and direct instruction.	Write a biography of your famous person. Use the timeline you created to help you organize your ideas. Remember to answer the following questions as you write. • When and where was your famous person born? • Where did your person live while growing up? • What was his or her childhood like? • What did your person do as an adult? • Why is your person famous?
Tier 2 These students can organize ideas without too much prompting.	Write a biography of your famous person. Use your timeline to help you organize your ideas. Remember to emphasize why your person is famous.
Tier 3 These students thrive on high levels of challenge.	Tell the reader about your famous person's life through a series of letters written over his or her lifespan from that person to a friend.

Figure 6.2. Sample tiered activity as part of a social studies unit.

Tiered Math Activity: Mean, Median, and Mode

Learning Goal: Students will understand data by using the mean, median, mode, and range to describe data sets

Below Grade Level	On Grade Level	Above Grade Level
Find the mean, median, and mode for the set of numbers: 2, 2, 3, 6, 7.	Find the mean, median, and mode for the set of numbers: 12, 5, 9, 8, 15, 24, 8, 5.	The mean is 5, the mode is 4, the median is 4. Generate number sets where this answer is possible.

Figure 6.3. Sample tiered math activity.

average-achieving student in a math class studying mean, median, and mode would typically be assigned the "On Grade Level" problem in Figure 6.3. Students who understand that their assigned task is a "minimum challenge" would be free to attempt the challenge of the above-grade-level task. Any time a student is willing to take on a challenge, she or he should be encouraged to do so.

Mr. Harper's fourth-grade students were beginning to study electricity. He distributed batteries, wires, and bulbs to his students and asked, "How can you make the bulb light?" Within minutes he had determined that seven of his students had mastered the concept of circuits. He pulled those seven students aside, gave them more wire and another bulb and asked, "Can you figure out how to light both bulbs so that when one bulb is removed the other will still stay lit?" Mr. Harper's pre-assessment lasted less than five minutes and his preparation for the tiered activity was minimal. Yet he provided appropriate challenge and activities to engage his students.

Tiered assignments can be short- or long-term activities. The students in Ms. Gorden's class—consisting of one cluster each of high-achieving, average-achieving, and low-achieving fourth-grade students—were studying the United States. Each student had written to a different state Chamber of Commerce and received tourism brochures. Ms. Gorden decided to try a new approach to her traditional state report. Her low-achieving students used a series of books on the states that were heavily illustrated along with text that was at the students' reading level. The average-achieving students used materials at grade level. And the high-achieving students used the travel brochures for their content. Ms. Gorden gave all the students the following directions:

> You work for a company that has asked you to transfer to the state
> you have been studying. They have sent you travel information in

an effort to help you learn about your potential new home. Create a list of the types of information that would be important to you if you were going to move to a new state. What information can you use from the brochures? What other information do you need to make an informed decision? Where might you find more facts to help you? Write a report on what you discover.

ANCHOR ACTIVITIES

When high-achieving students finish an assignment, they are often told to read, color, or are given additional work of the same difficulty level to keep them busy. It doesn't take children long to learn that finishing work leads to more of the same work; thus, they often choose not to finish their work or they become behavior problems (Colangelo, Assouline, & Gross, 2004; Reis, Gentry, & Park, 1995). Anchor activities are designed to keep students actively engaged in activities worthy of their time and appropriate to their learning needs (Tomlinson, 2001). Although anchor activities do not have to relate directly to the curriculum at hand, teachers can use anchor activities to provide students with meaningful work related to specific instructional goals. For example, if the class is studying government, then the anchor activity can serve as an extension to this social studies unit or focus on a skill such as understanding the difference between primary and secondary sources. They are self-paced, purposeful, ongoing activities on which students work independently. They may be short-term or long-term, ranging from a list of options from which students can choose each day to a multiple-week project.

Ms. Collins, the gifted and talented resource teacher in a large elementary school, realized shortly after accepting her new position that many of the gifted students were spending a good portion of their school day reading for pleasure or tutoring other students. Being sensitive to the materials the teachers were already using in the classroom for enrichment, she used other resources and assembled a series of logic problems, critical thinking activities, figural and verbal analogies, and creative thinking activities at each grade level. Most teachers laminated the activities on cards, a few made copies, and all created an Anchor Activities Learning Center for their classrooms. With these centers in place, Ms. Collins then started working with teams of teachers to develop a variety of more comprehensive activities that directly related to the curriculum.

The second-grade teachers developed a tiered anchor activity for their students to supplement the social studies unit. They introduced the activity to all of the students during a whole class lesson on natural resources. Each student had a two-pocket portfolio with specific instructions in one pocket and a place to keep their work in the other pocket. The students kept the portfolio in their desks and pulled them out to work on after they completed their classwork. The teachers developed three different prompts appropriate for the different achievement levels in their classrooms (see Figure 6.4). Students were assigned one of the three prompts based on their current level of achievement and the need for additional challenge in the classroom. Students who tended to have more independent work-time available due to the speed at which they completed their classwork were assigned Prompt 1, as the open-ended nature of that assignment required the most time to complete.

In all of these scenarios, the students were working on interesting tasks related to the same learning goal. While the basic content did not differ, the depth and complexity (Kaplan, in press) of the application of the content to the product varied relative to student readiness. Moreover, in all of the lessons, the high-achieving students were not asked to do more than the other students. Rather, they were asked to use different materials, create a different product, or engage in different tasks—a much more inviting and motivating practice than the more traditional "add to" approach.

By implementing anchor activities, curriculum compacting, and tiered activities teachers can begin to set the stage for a differentiated classroom. Such a classroom will reflect a variety of activities for a range of students and thus encourage maximum achievement from students who perform at varying levels of achievement.

Anchoring Activity: Natural Resources

Learning Goal: Students will learn about natural resources that are renewable and non-renewable.

Grade: 2

Overview: The 2nd-grade students have begun a unit about natural resources. Students may work individually or in small groups. This tiered activity with three prompts is designed to supplement the classroom unit. Prompt 1 is for students who benefit from a fair amount of structure in their learning activities. Prompt 2 is for students who work well independently when they are given specific guidelines. Prompt 3 is designed for students who are comfortable as independent learners.

Prompt 1: Our school custodians have a problem. Each day they throw out a large amount of paper. They would like to save as many trees as possible and would like to come up with a plan to recycle the paper used in the classrooms. Your job is to come up with a plan for the custodians.

Step 1:	With a partner, talk to the custodians to find out what they do with the paper now. Ask them if they have any ideas about how to solve the problem.
Step 2:	With your group, brainstorm ideas for solving the paper problem.
Step 3:	Use the PMI (Plus, Minus, Interesting) strategy that we have used in class to sort your ideas
Step 4:	Come up with 2 different plans using your "Plus" ideas.
Step 5:	Write up your 2 plans for the custodians.

Prompt 2: Every day our custodians throw out a tremendous amount of trash. What can we do at our school to reduce the amount of trash we throw out each day? Think about these different types of trash:
• Paper   • Food
• Plastic   • Cans and other metals
Come up with a plan that you can present to the principal that explains your solution to our trash problem.

Prompt 3: Every day our custodians throw out a tremendous amount of trash. What can we do at our school to reduce the amount of trash we throw out each day? Come up with a plan that you can present to the principal that explains your solution to our trash problem.

Figure 6.4. Sample anchoring activity.

7

INQUIRY-BASED INSTRUCTIONAL STRATEGIES

Children are naturally curious, and inquiry-based instructional strategies are designed to build their inquisitive nature. Questioning strategies, open-ended activities, problem-based learning, and independent and small group investigations are strategies included in this chapter that require students to become active seekers of knowledge and to take charge of their own learning.

QUESTIONING

"I have no answers, only questions." Socrates, c. 300 BC

Effective use of questioning can enhance learning (Gall, 1970; Graesser & Person, 1994; Kloss, 1988). But teachers tend to ask low-level questions, regardless of the ability or achievement level of the student (Gall, 1970; Hestenes, Cassidy, & Niemeyer, 2006; Mills, Rice, Berliner, & Rousseau 1980). Approximately 20% of the questions that teachers ask are procedural, and 60% require students to recall information. Only 20% of teachers' questions require students to think (Gall, 1970). How dull! Questions should encourage students to ponder, speculate, connect disparate facts and information, compare and contrast, and make judgments.

Asking Questions: Teachers

Asking students open-ended questions is a highly effective strategy; it requires students to think and provides differentiation. Students are often caught off-guard by questions that have no "right" answer since the vast majority of questions asked in school seek simple, one-right-answer information recall. The shift from asking a closed question to asking an open-ended question can be subtle: "Do you think the heat caused the change in this experiment?" to "What do you think caused the change in this experiment?" Listening to the first question, students are inclined think, "She asked about the heat, so that must be it." The question can be answered with a simple "yes" or "no." The revised question takes thought as the student is not led toward a simple answer or conclusion. Open-ended questions

⁕ have no "right" answer,

⁕ cause students to ask even more questions,

⁕ create a "discuss and debate" atmosphere,

⁕ invite reflection,

⁕ encourage students to make connections between ideas and disciplines,

⁕ encourage students to develop a conceptual understanding of the content area,

⁕ result in students thinking about their thinking,

⁕ foster critical and creative thinking, and

⁕ result in a broad range of responses.

Although students may originally be resistant to "having to think," as teachers increase their use of open-ended questions, students will be more willing to participate and take risks. Allowing ample wait time is essential when asking open-ended questions. It takes time to think of possible solutions. In addition, when teachers ask closed-ended questions, many students do not even try to think of answers as they are confident that other students will respond quickly. It takes many moments of awkward silence for these students to realize that no one else is answering the question and that it might be worth the effort to think about an answer. In Table 7.1, we list closed questions typically asked in classrooms and suggest wording to transform these questions into open-ended inquiries. With practice, asking open-ended questions can become second nature, resulting in students becoming deeper thinkers.

Asking Questions: Students

Students need to have the opportunity and be given the time to ask questions. They have no trouble thinking of closed questions, but often need to be taught how to ask open-ended questions. Mr. LaRue's students have gathered in a circle on the floor of the classroom. Sitting cross-legged in the midst of his 2nd-graders, Mr. LaRue asks, "Who can tell me what the word 'question' means?" Lakeesha quickly thrusts her hand in the air and says, "It's what you just did!" Tucker nodded in approval and adds, "You just asked us a question; it's what you do when you want to know something." After a brief discussion Mr. LaRue asked, "How many legs

Table 7.1. Closed and Corresponding Open-ended Questions.

Closed Questions	Open-ended Questions
Do you think the character did the right thing?	How do you feel about the character's actions?
What did the character do when . . . ?	What might the character have done instead of . . . ?
How did the character solve his problem?	How would you have solved the problem if you were the character?
Is multiplication repeated addition?	How are multiplication and addition related?
According to the book, what were the causes of the Civil War?	If you were living in the South during this time, why might you have felt the need to go to war?
What is a milkmaid?	What might a milkmaid be?
What happened when . . . ?	What do you think might happen if . . . ?
What is 6 x 7?	If the answer is 42, what is the question?
Which artist painted this picture?	What do you know by looking at this picture?
What happened when . . . ?	What would be different if . . . ?
Do you think the character did the right thing?	How do you feel about the character's actions?

do you have?" Hands shot up around the room, and Aubrey blurted out, "Two!" Mr. LaRue then asked, "How would your life be different if you had three legs?" The reaction to this question was very different as students sat contemplating their answers while Mr. LaRue wrote both questions on the flip chart. Mr. LaRue interrupted his students' thinking with a comment, "I just asked you two different types of questions. One was a fat question, and one was a very skinny question. Which question (pointing to the two questions on the flip chart) do you think was fat? Which one was skinny?" Mackenzie scrunched up her nose and slowly raised her hand, "I think the three legs question is fat because it takes up a lot of space in your brain to think of an answer. The two legs one is skinny because it hardly takes up any thinking space." Eyes lit up in recognition as Mackenzie's classmates started nodding their heads in agreement. Mr. LaRue said, "Using Mackenzie's idea, can someone ask a skinny question?" Nahyr, a budding veterinarian, asked, "How many gerbils do we have in our room?" Greg, who always seemed eager to go home, asked, "What time does school end?" Cecelia, dressed in her usual pink dress and shoes, asked with a grin, "What is my favorite color?" Mr. LaRue asked how much thinking space those questions took in their brains and the class agreed that they took very little. The class moved on to consider fat questions. After sharing the answers to the "three-leg question," they were amazed at the variety of answers. Sierra observed, "Our answers are all different!" Mr. LaRue said, "That is exactly what makes a fat question a fat question!" Students then practiced asking fat questions, which they discovered was more difficult, but much more fun and interesting than asking skinny questions.

Mr. LaRue's second graders had just taken their first steps toward becoming question finders. Being able to ask questions of others and about situations is an essential skill for life-long learning. Learning to pose thoughtful questions is an integral step in critical and creative thinking processes and helps set the stage for a rich life of inquiry. The difference between fat and skinny questions can be subtle. Compare, "How did he solve the problem?" to "How might he have solved the problem?" Changing one word has turned a recall question into one that requires higher levels of thought. See Table 7.2 for "question starters" that differentiate between fat and skinny questions.

Questioning to Differentiate

By their very nature, open-ended questions differentiate. These questions require students to think, and they target readiness levels as students synthesize prior knowledge and information gained from the classroom activity to answer the question at their level of understanding. A child in the high-achieving cluster

Table 7.2. Skinny and Fat Question Starters.

Skinny Question Starters	Fat Question Starters
How many . . . ?	How many...? How might . . .?
Who was . . . ?	Who was...? Who should . . . ?
When did . . . ?	When did...? When might . . .?
What is . . . ?	Predict . . .
Can . . . ?	Why do you think . . . ?
Where did . . .?	Where might . . . ?
Did . . . ?	In what ways...?
Will . . . ?	What do you think about . . . ?
Do you agree/disagree with...?	Why you agree/disagree with . . . ?
How did...?	What advice would you give . . . ?
What did...?	What else could . . . ?

may go through a detailed explanation of photosynthesis during a discussion about plants, whereas another child may simply explain that plants need sun and water to survive. All children can contribute, and all contributions are respected.

Whether students achieve at the high, average, or low levels, there will be times when an open-ended question is ineffective with certain students. At those times, these children may need to be asked a more direct question. As teachers come to understand their students' strengths, interests, and learning profiles, they learn how to use different types of questions to differentiate instructions for their students. As with any differentiation strategy, the key is in maintaining a variety of techniques.

OPEN-ENDED ACTIVITIES

Open-ended activities develop critical and creative thinking skills and help students become better problem solvers. These activities encourage divergent, critical, and creative thinking as there are endless possible solutions. The challenge level with open-ended activities is fluid as students respond from their own achievement level and experience. In addition, as students work more independently, motivation and persistence increase and attitudes improve (Van Deur, 2003).

On Monday morning Mrs. Haines wrote "27" on the assignment board in her third-grade classroom. Her students had the answer, now they needed to create the problem. Over the next four days, they needed to develop five different problems so that the answer to each problem equaled 27. The variety of the problems that the students created reflected the diverse achievement levels in the classroom. Greg, who struggled with mathematical concepts, wrote the following problems:

$26 + 1 = 27$

$3 \times 9 = 27$

$30 - 3 = 27$

$25 + 2 = 27$

$24 + 3 = 27$

His success in finding five correct solutions boosted his confidence, and the next time Mrs. Haines gave the number of the week and requested five problems, he developed eight problems.

Reagan, identified as average-achieving and always the last to complete her multiplication timed-test, wrote the following problem:

> Thaddeus, Alexandria, and Cleopatra were all students in Mrs.
> Hayes' 3rd grade classroom in the year 1987 and that year they all had

some marbles. Alexandria had twice as many marbles as Thaddeus, which made Thaddeus very jealous. Thaddeus had 2 red marbles and some multi-colored marbles. Cleopatra had 3 fewer marbles than Alexandria and 4 of hers were her favorite color, green. How many marbles did each child have if the total number of marbles that all of the children had was less than 50 and a multiple of 9?

Reagan did not enjoy computation exercises out of the textbook, but thoroughly enjoyed writing complex problems that required critical thinking and a much higher level of computation than the exercises in the textbook. Mrs. Haines forgave her for only providing one problem due to the obvious complexity of her question. (See the end of the chapter for the answer.)

Turning a closed problem or activity into an open-ended one does not always require extensive preparation. In Table 7.3 we provide examples of typical questions that have been slightly altered to increase the level of challenge. Also included are suggestions for scaffolding the problem for students who struggle with material that does not have "one right answer." We believe that for every closed-ended, one-right-answer problem given to students another open-ended problem should also be given to them, and in doing so, teachers will help students learn to think.

PROBLEM-BASED LEARNING

Problem-based learning (PBL) is a form of open-ended learning that involves more in-depth study (Gallagher & Stepien, 1996). It differentiates content and process while encouraging active learning through the exploration of a real-world problem. The goal of problem-based learning is to have students act like junior practicing professionals. They approach problem solving as do the experts in the field, confronting situations that do not have specific answers. Students gain content knowledge and acquire skills while becoming more proficient problem solvers and critical thinkers. Students are only given guidelines, not assigned specific tasks, as the teacher takes on the role of facilitator rather than instructor. Assessment is authentic and performance-based as students develop solutions to real problems.

Mrs. Scanlon's second- and third-grade class attacked their PBL activity with such enthusiasm that she wasn't sure they would ever stop their inquiry. In Ms. Scanlon's words:

It started one fine Monday afternoon. After studying the rainforest and causes of deforestation, I posed this question to my class, "What can you do to help the environment?" Throughout the unit, I challenged the kiddos not to think of rainforest deforestation as someone else's problem many miles away. I asked them to commit to helping the environment locally. I asked them to consider what they were doing to aid the environment as they called on others to put an end to earth-unfriendly behaviors. Their responses to the essential question and their plans of action were inspiring.

Ms. Scanlon's students decided to complete several group projects. They shared the information they learned through a website designed to create awareness, a newscast to their school, and a display of information gathered through surveying area schools about their earth-friendly practices. They also started a fund-raising campaign through a recycling effort and by developing animal trading cards. The students used

Table. 7.3. Closed Activities, Open Activities, and Possible Scaffolds.

Closed Activity	Open Activity	Scaffold Options
Which of these spinners is fair?	Draw a fair and unfair spinner.	What makes a spinner fair?
Write a summary of the book.	Write about the surprises you found in the book.	Brainstorm interesting moments in the book.
Make $1.00 using the fewest coins.	How many ways can you make $1.00 using coins?	Use play money.
Create a diorama of the habitat of a bear.	Create an imaginary woodland mammal and make a diorama of a habitat in which your creature could survive.	Develop a list of characteristics of woodland mammals prior to creating a new mammal.
You have 2 quarters, 3 dimes, 1 nickel, and 2 pennies; can you make 72 cents?	Using 2 quarters, 3 dimes, 1 nickel, and 2 pennies; make as many different amounts of money as you can.	Do you have to use all of the coins each time?
Worksheet of addition problems.	How many different ways can you add numbers to get a sum of 15?	Blanks: ____ + ____ = 15 ____ + ____ + ____ = 15
Write a book report.	Be a critic and write a book review.	Outline

the proceeds to purchase acres of land in the rainforest through a conservation trust. Asking one open-ended, meaningful question resulted in an impressive learning outcome for the students, one that held personal meaning for them. When children learn early that through education they can make a difference, then we help educate a future generation of people who can think, act, and become productive members of our democracy. As John Dewey said, "The process of education should be thus conceived as the process of learning to think through the solutions of real problems" (Dewey, 1916).

Independent Study and Small Group Investigation

Student interest can lead to highly effective independent investigations. Working in an area of passion often results in motivated and self-directed students. Students (individually or in small groups) identify a topic of interest or problem to solve, narrow the focus so that the agenda is manageable, plan an investigation, and culminate the study with a product that they share with interested audiences (Renzulli & Reis, 1997). Despite the fact that these students are excited about these topics of interest, they don't always have the necessary skills to become successful independent learners. Mrs. Lisle developed forms to help guide her students through the process. When a student expresses interest in exploring a topic, she meets briefly with the student to discuss the Independent Study Plan (see Figure 7.1 and Appendix A). Over the years, she has found that the most difficult part of the process for students is to narrow the focus of their research. Mrs. Lisle discovered

Independent Study Plan			
Name			
Teacher			
Beginning Date			
Estimated Ending Date			
General Areas of Study (check all that apply)			
Science	Language Arts	Social Studies	Art
Math	Music	Other	
What is the topic of your study?			
What do you hope to find out?			
List three things you will do to get started.			
1.			
2.			
3.			
Teacher Verification Section: Student has completed above three tasks. (teacher signature)			
List the resources you will use during your study (books, Internet sites, magazines, videos, maps, people, etc.)			
What form will your final product take?			
With whom will you share your product?			

Figure 7.1. Independent study plan.

that many of her students would express an interest in working on an independent study, but only a few persevere. As a result she added, "List 3 things you will do to get started." After answering that question as well as "What do you hope to find out?" Mrs. Lisle sends the student to the library to locate three resources (e.g. a book, a website, and an individual to interview). Students list those three resources and then come back to see her. This step is enough to weed out those students who are not committed to following through with the project. The students who do return with their resources listed then complete the study plan and begin their research. The Independent Study Log (see Figure 7.2 and Appendix A) helps students focus their efforts. Each week the student sets three goals. As the week progresses, students carry out their research during time they earn through compacting the curriculum or streamlining instruction. Once each week Mrs. Lisle sits down with the student to review progress on the goals and help him or her set goals for the following week. When the student finishes the project, he or she completes the Independent Study Presentation Form (see Figure 7.3 and Appendix A) and identifies an audience. Some students present to previous year's teachers, and others present to authentic audiences. To assess the project, students then use

---

INDEPENDENT STUDY LOG

Name _____
Teacher _____
Date _____
Project Title _____

My three goals:
1. _____
2. _____
3. _____

Reflection:
Did I accomplish my goals? _____

What did I do well? _____
_____
_____
_____

What could I have done better? _____
_____
_____
_____

Next week I will . . . Record three goals for the next week on your next log sheet.

Figure 7.2. Independent study log.

INDEPENDENT STUDY PRESENTATION FORM
I AM READY TO PRESENT!

Name _____
Teacher _____
Date _____
Project Title _____

I would like to present my project to the following classes or groups:
_____
_____
_____

The length of my presentation is approximately _____

I will require the following equipment: _____
_____
_____

I need to remember to take the following papers and materials with me: _____
_____
_____

The best time of day for me to present my project is: _____

Figure 7.3. Independent study presentation form.

INDEPENDENT STUDY STUDENT EVALUATION

Name
Teacher
Topic of Study
Project Title

What do you think was the best thing about your independent study?

Now that you have more experience, what are some things you would do better or in a different way?

What are some questions that you still have about your topic?

What suggestions would you have for another student who is interested in doing an independent study?

Figure 7.4 Independent study evaluation form.

the Independent Study Evaluation (see Figure 7.4 and Appendix A) after completing their product presentations.

Independent studies are particularly powerful when a student has a real audience to whom she or he can report results. Latrell and Jasmine were dismayed to see the amount of food thrown away each day at lunch. Although they had seen other students do independent study projects on topics such as the Civil War and Shakespeare, they asked Mrs. Lisle if they could explore something that they didn't feel was "school stuff."

They researched different ways in which they might measure food waste in their cafeteria. When they settled on a method, Latrell arranged a visit with the cafeteria manager. After gathering food waste for a week, they reported their findings to the manager. The manager was so impressed with their findings that she worked with Latrell and Jasmine to create an awareness campaign about food waste. Jasmine and Latrell continued to work on their project for the remaining three months of school. They were so enthusiastic about the reduction in food waste that occurred after their campaign that they arranged to meet with the superintendent to inform her of their progress and suggest that she institute their program at other schools in the district. They were amazed at her enthusiasm and thrilled to be "Food Waste Reduction Ambassadors" to other schools.

The sense of social justice can be very high in gifted children (Robinson, Reis, Neihart, & Moon,, 2002). Often their interests exist in areas where they see a problem and are desperate to remedy the situation. Real world projects, such as Latrell and Jasmine's, that result in student making a difference in their world are particularly effective. Renzulli (2002) discussed the need to promote social capital in children:

Can educators imagine a role for schools that will influence the leaders of the new century in ways that will help them acquire values that produce social capital as well as material consumption and economic gain? Can a vision about the role of education include creating future political leaders who place fairness and kindness and social justice ahead of power, control, and pandering to special interests? And can we create the future CEOs of automobile and energy companies who are as committed to safety and emission control as they are to shareholders' profits, sexier cars, and the corporate bottom line? Could some of the endless pitches for commercial products at least be interspersed with advocacy for more time with our children, a greater tolerance for diversity, and more concern for the rapid depletion of the Earth's resources? It is intriguing to think that the men and women who will decide the content of such messages are the boys and girls who are in our classrooms today. (p. 57)

The leaders to whom Renzulli referred—who advocate for safety, environmental responsibility, and tolerance—undoubtedly acquired these values as children. They may not have started with monumental projects, but rather with small personal ones. Latrell and Jasmine were concerned about food waste and acted on the problem.

Nicholas mentioned to Ms. Richardson, his first-grade teacher, that the brown patch of dirt outside their classroom window "looked very boring and needed something." Rather than waiting for someone else to solve the problem, he suggested a solution to his teacher. With Ms. Richardson's help and a bit of help from his mother, he researched indigenous plants, talked to the manager of a local nursery, and developed a landscaping plan for the 48-square-foot plot of land. After visiting the nursery, he realized that he would need funding to follow through on his plan. Nicholas' excitement about the project was contagious and when he met with the principal to share his idea, she volunteered to match the funds that he raised. Nicholas decided to hold a bake sale at school and recruited two friends who "really understood how to handle money" to help him during the sale. He wrote a note to send home with the students in his class requesting bake sale items, and he and his parents made "mountains of rice krispie treats and cookies." The entire first-grade class helped Nicholas plant the garden, and the students happily took turns watering it daily for the first few weeks. While some people might view this activity as being outside of the curriculum, the amount of learning far exceeded the first-grade standards. Nicholas learned about plants, how they reproduce, the difference between perennials and annual flowers, the need for some plants to have full sunlight and others shade, and why different plants require different types of soil. Nicholas used mathematics constantly as he dealt with measurement when determining heights of different plants and distances between plants, currency when raising money and purchasing plants, fractions when helping his parents bake, and multiplication and number sense as they doubled and tripled recipes. He also worked on his communication and interpersonal skills through his meetings with the principal and nursery manager, his letter requesting donations for the bake sale, and his supervision of his classmates during the bake sale and garden planting. The enthusiasm for this project did not fade once it was completed. The satisfaction of seeing the fruits of his labor resulted in Nicholas supervising the maintenance of the garden through fifth grade. Each year the first graders in Ms. Richardson's class took responsibility for replacing plants as necessary, weeding, and watering the garden. They used the opportunity to study the life cycle of plants. When Nicholas was in middle school he was inspired by an Arbor Day celebration and began a tree-planting campaign in his community.

According to Renzulli (2002), traits that promote social capital "develop when students become passionately involved in an area of personal choice" (p. 39). When students are provided with opportunities to work in their areas of interest, they not only learn academic skills, but also learn about themselves and develop characteristics that promote social capital. The book *The Kids' Guide to Social Action* (Lewis, 1998) provides a step-by-step guide to social action skills for children and serves as an excellent resource for teachers and students interested in making a difference.

ENSURING CHALLENGE

Raising the bar for all students is essential in order to prepare our children for the real world. Our work with cluster grouping (Gentry & Owen, 1999) and enrichment clusters (Renzulli, Gentry, & Reis, 2003) revealed some specific strategies used by teachers to ensure the delivery of challenging curriculum and instruction. The checklist in Figure 7.5 (and Appendix A) offers teachers the opportunity to consider using and implementing research-based strategies to increase challenge and rigor in the curriculum. We encourage you to take a few minutes to reflect on how frequently you incorporate these strategies into your daily teaching.

SUMMARY

Differentiated instruction comes in many forms. The strategies discussed here represent just a few of the effective instructional differentiation techniques that can

STRATEGIES FOR ENSURING CHALLENGE				
	Frequency of Use			
Strategy	Consistently	Often	Occasionally	Never
Introduce new concepts				
Present advanced content and consult advanced resources				
Develop products and services				
Use authentic methods and tools				
Use advanced vocabulary				
Integrate creative thinking				
Consider historical perspectives				
Engage students in presentations and performances				
Respond to student interests				
Encourage student directed learning and choice				
Focus on problem solving, critical and creative thinking				
Provide curricular extensions and enrichments				
Use open-ended questions and activities				
Implement curriculum compacting and give credit to students who meet standards				
Adjust assignments based on student's skill level				
Provide many choices				

Figure 7.5. Chart for ensuring challenge in classroom activities.

be used to provide an appropriate level of challenge to all students. Anchoring activities, compacting, tiered activities, open-ended activities, problem-based learning, independent studies, and varying questions work particularly well in cluster-grouped classrooms. These techniques should be considered a starting point in the differentiation journey. There are many other quality resources that can be used to help educators continue to augment and refine their differentiation repertoire.

Other techniques that were not discussed here, but can be found in the resources listed in Appendix B, include Think-Tac-Toe (Roberts & Inman, 2007), varying journal prompts, learning contracts, learning centers, interest centers, and mentorships. Regardless of the strategy used, the hallmark of differentiation in the cluster grouped classroom is flexible grouping. The students in the high-achieving cluster should not spend all of their time working together. Pre-assessment is essential to ensure appropriate placement of students in curricular lessons for them to master the content and, hopefully, exceed the grade-level standards. Interest-based groupings should also be used on a regular basis, which will result in mixed-achievement groups of highly motivated students focused on an area of common interest.

The annotated resources list in Appendix B contains materials to help you on your differentiation journey. There are many books available and websites full of information on differentiation. We have attempted to save you some time wading through the available material by making a few recommendations. No matter what resource you use or what strategies you try, just remember to take small steps, not giant leaps. Do not attempt to change everything you are doing over the weekend. Try one strategy for one lesson and build from there. Conserve your preparation time by rallying your colleagues and working with them to develop and share different activities. Discover what works well for you as a teacher and for your students and develop activities that fit with your teaching style and their learning profiles. Every differentiated classroom will look a little different, and that is exactly the point of differentiation!

Reagan's Answer to Her Marble Question

Thaddeus m	Alexandria 2 x m	Cleopatra (2 x m) – 3	Total	
1	1	-		Impossible
2	4	1	7	
3	6	3	12	
4	8	5	17	• Must be between 7 and 47
5	10	7	22	
6	12	9	27	• Must be a multiple of 9
7	14	11	32	• 27 is the only multiple of 9
8	16	13	35	
9	18	15	42	
10	20	17	47	
11	22	19	52	Too large

Thaddeus has 6 marbles
Alexandria has 12 marbles
Cleopatra has 9 marbles
Together they have 27 marbles

8

STUDENT-FOCUSED DIFFERENTIATION

Differentiation centers on providing quality education to students based on their various educational needs, which include their strengths, weaknesses, readiness, skill levels, interests, and learning preferences (Roberts & Inman, 2007; Tomlinson, 1999). School mission statements frequently reflect the duty of schools to prepare youth for the future and to contribute to the maximum educational growth of individual children—goals best achieved through effective differentiation practices. Most schools have mission statements similar to the following:

> *It is the mission of Happy Elementary School to educate each individual child to help him or her reach his or her fullest potential for life-long learning in a diverse democracy.*

These mission statements contain quality ideas. Yet too often school practices that deliver locked-step content based on one-size-fits-all standards run contrary to this mission. Quite simply, we must consider whether children are the same as or different from one another. By acknowledging their differences, we can begin to use cluster grouping and differentiated practices to address their individual learning needs.

Rather than emphasizing and measuring how students achieve when compared to other students, we ought to focus on how much they individually improve. What has each child learned during the school year based on where he or she began in the fall? Children start school in different places, with different levels of readiness and experiences and with different beliefs about their ability to succeed in the tasks being asked of them in school. When test scores are used to compare one group of students to another without regard to where they began, educators are, in effect, held accountable for factors out of their control. How often or whether parents read to their children, the developmental readiness of the child, the child's past failures or successes, how much the child lost or gained over the summer, and the value a family places on education all affect students' achievement in school. Moreover, by paying attention to where the child begins, we can assess how much he or she learns during the school year. We can adjust the curriculum and instruction to a level that encourages learning and success for the child. And we can become accountable for individual gains.

As discussed in Part 1, when we cluster-group children, we do so to increase the teachers' ability to address the varied individual needs of her students. Clustering reduces the range of achievement levels in each teacher's classroom, and it provides teachers with groups of students who achieve at or near the same level. The initial grouping provides a beginning point for differentiation; however without differentiation, no reason exists to cluster students.

In addition to teacher-directed efforts toward differentiation, what we call "student-focused" strategies offer teachers a means of increasing student motivation, creativity, and ownership in their learning. In effect, the student-focused strategies offer a different approach to more traditional curricular differentiation discussed in Chapters 6 and 7. This menu does not represent a one-size-fits-all list of things that teachers must do, but rather a collection of effective practices borrowed from great teachers around the country, from the teachers in our research, and from our own experiences. Specifically, these student-focused practices are designed to help teachers turn the learning back to the students and to help students take responsibility for their own learning. Thus, they provide teachers a quick start to differentiation because they often require less work and planning on the part of the teacher. Moreover, these strategies engage students in individualized rigor, depth, and complexity based on genuine interest, and in doing so, they develop creativity, buy-in, work-ethic, and engage students (Kaplan, in press; Kaplan & Cannon, 2001).

In the following paragraphs we outline 25 strategies. Take some ideas, try them, and adjust (differentiate) them to your own strengths, needs, and styles. Most importantly, use these strategies to help your students take charge of their learning in a meaningful manner. When used frequently, these strategies can help teachers create learning environments in which being smart is considered cool by the students!

MENU OF STUDENT-FOCUSED STRATEGIES

1 **Offer students the opportunity to do fewer, but more difficult problems.** This simple approach can be highly motivating to students of all achievement levels, and it works across the curriculum. In language arts, students can answer a dozen comprehension questions about the reading, or they could respond to two questions (that require comprehension) that ask them to respond in-depth using higher-order thinking skills to more abstract literary components such as theme, voice, or characterization. In mathematics, students might choose to complete three story problems or 20 computation problems, or they might create their own problems and answer key. Offer this option often enough, and students will actually begin to ask if they can have fewer but harder problems!

2 **Share yourself and encourage the same from your students.** Students who know each other and who know the teacher provide the foundation for a responsive classroom (Rimm-Kaufmann & Sawyer, 2004). When kids know and understand each other and when respect for individual differences is encouraged, they are less likely to bully or be bullied, and they develop a rapport in the classroom that is supportive of their peers (Peterson, 2003; Peterson & Ray, 2006a; Peterson & Ray, 2006b). In a supportive environment, students feel safe to take risks—an essential element of academic growth and creativity—and students can make mistakes without fear of ridicule and thus learn from those mistakes (Rimm-Kaufmann & Sawyer, 2004). Finally, when students know each other's interests, those interests can be effectively integrated into the educational content.

3 **Ask the students what will work.** As a teacher, I (Gentry) often encountered situations in which what I was trying to do with the kids failed miserably. As a beginning teacher, I found these instances extremely frustrating. Despite my best efforts to prepare an engaging lesson, the students seemed to find the lesson dull, boring, and uneventful. And I had just put hours into planning! During one of these disappointing lessons on photosynthesis, I finally, out of desperation, asked the students, "What do you think would work to teach this concept to you guys?" I was astounded when I received about a half-dozen really great suggestions. I had given the students the terms, a diagram, and (what I considered to be) thought-provoking questions. They suggested that we become the water, sunlight, carbon dioxide, glucose, and oxygen. So we did, and they learned the content. In fact, fourth graders were able to balance the photosynthetic equation. They did so by becoming molecules of water, complete with two hydrogen atoms duct-taped to an oxygen atom. Since then, asking the students what would work has provided me with more free time, as well as let loose my creative energies as I listen to and respond to their ideas. I believe that encouraging their voices in the classroom leads to greater ownership by students of the learning activities.

4 **Laugh, care, appreciate energy, creativity, and humor.** Like strategy No. 2, this strategy holds the promise of creating an inviting and safe learning environment. Laughter and humor can carry students and teachers through even the most difficult of days. Humor is a sign of creativity and can add enjoyment to the classroom. Overexcitabilities (Dabrowski, 1972) in gifted children, including psychomotor, sensual, imaginational, emotional, and intellectual have been discussed (Piechowski, 1985). These intensities can be misunderstood and mistaken for weaknesses rather than signs of talent among young children. For example, sometimes adults consider a child to be hyperactive when in fact she is simply delightfully energetic and in need of physical and mental stimulation. Similarly, what may appear to be a deficit in attention might really be an indication of a child who is mentally very busy. Sometimes bright students will have "different" senses of humor and seeing their humor as an asset rather than a liability can lead to recognition of talent among these students. Research and practice have shown that there is an increase in misdiagnosis of disorders such as ADHD based on a misunderstanding of behaviors (Eide & Eide, 2006; Webb et al, 2005). Gates (2007) found in her study of the co-occurence of giftedness with ADHD and the potential misdiagnosis of giftedness as ADHD that some rating scales for ADHD and giftedness have as much as an 80% overlap of items. Thus, it depends on whether one is viewing the gift or the liability (Webb, 2000; Webb et al., 2005).

5 **Assess, incorporate, and develop student interests.** In Chapter 5, we devoted a section to describing the importance of learning about your students and their interests. As we learn about students' interests, these interests can be incorporated into the curriculum and serve as the basis for further independent investigations or extensions. Equally important to assessing and incorporating interests is developing them. Renzulli and Reis (1997) discussed using Type I activities to develop student interests. School should be a place where students learn and develop. Putting into place a plan to expose students to concepts and ideas with which they may not

be familiar helps develop new interests. This exposure is especially important for elementary students and for children who live in poverty, as their knowledge of and exposure to the world may more limited than that of older students or students from higher socio-economic backgrounds. Mrs. Rogers has a speaker come in to her fourth-grade classroom each week to share careers with her students. Mr. Smith selects a science show each month to stimulate students' interest about research in science and schedules field trips to nearby areas of educational interest.

6 **Be interesting in your teaching.** One sure-fire way to hold the interest of students is to keep them guessing. Some teachers tell stories, something Phenix (1964) referred to as artistic modification; others dress up in character; while still others put learning to song. Whatever it is that sets you apart from other teachers, that connects you with your students and brings your lessons to life—do that. We can all remember an interesting teacher, a teacher to whom we listened and from whom we learned. Many of us actually connect a specific content area to the teacher who taught it. This connection is strong evidence concerning the power of a teacher to bring content to life.

7 **Share your interests.** Mr. Cohen is interested in theater, he also coaches soccer and raises Boston Terriers. His shares his interests with his students, who eagerly await news of a new litter of puppies, try out for a part in the school musical, enjoy watching him in a community play, or seeing him on the sidelines of the recreational soccer league. By sharing his interests with his students, he serves as a model for the power of interests to enrich one's life. He also connects with the other theater-types, dog lovers, and soccer players in his class. He appreciates them, and they appreciate him. He is more than a teacher, he is a whole person to his students.

8 **Choose controversy.** Nothing can incite learning more than emotion. Most areas of study have controversial issues related to them. Controversy provides powerful learning opportunities because, by its very nature, it is multifaceted, open-ended, and it provides fuel for high-level debate. Should the wolves be taken off the endangered species list? Should farmers be allowed to use genetically modified animals in breeding? Should third graders be able to check Harry Potter out of the library? Should America provide resources to countries that violate the international moratorium on whaling? Can eating french fries cause cancer? When kids are still arguing at the end of the day about a controversial topic addressed before lunch, you have their attention. Often these kinds of topics afford opportunities to teach the finer skills of debate and to engage students in advanced content and process.

9 **Remember that students can produce knowledge.** Of all the strategies for differentiation, this one is probably used the least. In school, we teach children stuff, ask them to learn it, and occasionally, we even ask them to apply it. Rarely do we ask them to answer a previously unknown question: to produce knowledge. Yet, they are capable of doing that very thing, from writing an original, publishable story or poem to conducting a research project to which the answer is unknown. For example, Hunter Scott investigated, through original survey research, the circumstances surrounding the sinking of the SS Indianapolis in World War II (Nelson, 2002). Based on the accounts of remaining survivors, he testified before Congress and posthumously reversed the court marshal of the ship's captain. New knowledge. A fifth grader investigated the quality of the drinking fountain water in the school and five other public places. New knowledge. A group of second graders found out how much paper the school wasted in a day and developed a plan for recycling and re-using paper in the school. New knowledge. A sixth grader posed a question about whether freezing a tadpole would kill it (it won't; they have antifreeze in their cells). New knowledge. Students investigated truth in advertising and found that there weren't 1000 chips in every bag of chocolate chip cookies as advertised. New knowledge. Think about helping students learn to ask questions and find answers. What new knowledge might your students produce during the school year?

10 **Provide depth and complexity based on student questions and interests.** This strategy represents the opposite of teaching to the objective; rather it focuses on seizing the teachable moment and using student questions and interests as a basis for providing the depth. For example, Joshua stomped into the classroom one morning shortly after Hurricane Katrina had made landfall. "They shouldn't have messed with the Mississippi!" he exclaimed when Mr. Neville asked him what was on his mind. There was a look of confusion on the faces of many of Joshua's fellow fourth graders. Mr. Neville looked at the class and asked, "How might things have been different during Hurricane Katrina if people hadn't 'messed with the Mississippi'?" Mr. Neville planned to teach a wetlands unit in the spring, but his plans just changed. Joshua's passion about the impact of Hurricane Katrina developed into a problem-based learning activity. The students explored the effect that the levees and floodwalls had on the protective wetlands. They compared the Gulf Coast coastal wetlands to the New England inland wetlands. Mr. Neville was amazed at the extent of knowledge his students gained during their exploration. Joshua's outburst resulted in an investigation that far exceeded the grade level expectations for the wetlands unit.

11 **Take the time, jump in over your head, and start with a big-picture problem that students don't have all the skills or knowledge to solve.** Students often look to the teacher to know all the answers, especially in the elementary grades. However, equally as powerful as knowing all the answers is helping students learn to find answers to complex problems. As discussed in Chapter 7, the development of knowledge and skills in problem-based learning results from the need to acquire them to solve an urgent problem. Thus, jumping in the deep end, but with a flotation device that can help navigate those waters, can be an effective way to facilitate learning. It requires little preparation, an open mind, and the ability to see where the journey leads. Student and teacher can learn together. For example, an elementary student was very interested in equity, and she worried that a classmate who was wheelchair bound could not access the playground equipment. Clearly, neither she nor her teacher had the knowledge necessary to design, propose, raise funds, and build a new playground. They started small—just with an idea—worked with experts, and gained the knowledge and skills during the course of the project. The student's work resulted in the construction of a new, handicapped-accessible playground.

12 **Whenever possible, provide open-ended assignments; be ambiguous.** Students often want to know what, exactly, they need to do and what, exactly, is expected of them. They seek the one right answer to the closed-ended problems and assignments that dominate school-work and testing. Moreover, some high-achievers keep school exciting by seeing how quickly they can arrive at these right answers and finish their assignments. Unfortunately, closed-ended, one-right-answer problems do very little to develop the intellectual dispositions of children, "where risk-taking, exploration, uncertainty and speculation are what it's about" (Eisner, 2001, p. 368). By providing fewer details, less structure, and questions or problems that have multiple solutions, you encourage students to think and to struggle, cornerstones of intellectual development.

A favorite example of a totally ambiguous assignment involved a teacher who taught fossilization to her students. As a culminating project at the end of the unit, she told her students to "bring something in that demonstrates your understanding of fossilization." To raise the ante, she also awarded extra credit to students who added new content to their project. Tom brought in an ice-cube tray full of frozen tadpoles and suggested that he be given 20 extra credit points because, though they had learned about fossilization in sediment, in amber, and through petrification, no mention had been made of fossilization in ice. He went on to discuss ice mummification, antifreeze in frogs, and how preservation of remains has been of interest to humans for as long as there have been humans. Had this teacher assigned a poster with specific criteria, this student would not have been forced to engage his thinking, creativity, and to explore uncharted areas of the content that they had studied. Ambiguity often leads to much more than we could assign, and it also leads to a rich diversity in student responses. Finally, ambiguity takes less planning on the part of the teacher, saving valuable time for other tasks.

13 **Use challenge problems daily, weekly, monthly, and on tests and assignments.** These provide a low-risk way to elevate the level of advanced content, challenge students willing to attempt them, and create a classroom environment that supports intellectual risks and accomplishments. Teach above the standard. Tell students that the hard content will be on the test or assignment only as extra credit. Then encourage all students to attempt the challenging extra credit problems. These problems will motivate some of the students who may not consistently achieve at high levels, but who welcome a challenging problem. We have found that using challenge problems on tests that frustrate even the highest achieving students raises the bar for these students and provides a means of checking who understands the advanced concepts. This strategy is low-risk to students because they have nothing to lose, but they can gain extra points for their efforts in solving these challenge problems. We have even seen students begin to bring in challenge problems for the teachers to use or try to solve, reinforcing that being smart in this classroom is desirable.

14 **Begin at the back of the book.** Every elementary math book begins with number sense, place value, adding, subtracting, multiplying, and dividing whole numbers, then decimals, then fractions. Turn to the end of the math book and find the chapter on probability, which integrates all of the basic concepts in a much more interesting and relevant format. Additionally, find the chapter on geometry, which might excite some of the more concrete and spatial learners and which also uses basic operations. These last two chapters often go untouched or end up relegated to the very end of the school year. Try them first.

Likewise, language arts curricula typically deal with parts of speech, grammar, punctuation, sentence, then paragraph structure. Turn to the last chapters in the text and find exploration of different forms of writing and voice, followed by various purposes for writing. Each of these topics integrates the basic content found in the first chapters, but in a more engaging and authentic manner. Try these chapters first, or at the very least, pretest in the content areas to avoid the massive unengaging, repetition that occurs each year. Start with that which is interesting to the students whether they have the requisite skills or not, then build the skills through engaging them in the more interesting and relevant content.

15 **Ensure access to advanced content for all students.** Advanced content— the what, the why, the controversy, the unanswered questions, the "what is new" about a topic—can be extremely interesting. Typically, textbooks, educators, and curricula reserve the advanced content (if it is offered at all) for high-achieving students, and focus more on core content and basic skills with other students. However, like beginning at the back of the book, the advanced content can provide all students with context, meaning, and relevance for the basic knowledge. Not all students will engage in high-level projects based on the advanced content, but most students, even non-readers or those who always seem to be behind in their work, will find the advanced content interesting and be able to comprehend it. For many students, the interest stimulated by advanced content can play a role in increased motivation and offer a medium in which to deliver the basic knowledge and skills.

Just because teachers introduce advanced content, doesn't mean that they have to hold all students accountable for it. Rather, introduce it and let students learn what they can about it—learn for the sake of learning because it is interesting. Put questions about the advanced content on a test or quiz, but only for extra credit points. Make it cool to be smart and earn extra points by understanding the hard concepts. Teach difficult content to a level that ensures no students correctly answer all the extra credit questions. This provides a safe challenge (it is extra) and removes the ceiling for students who always get everything right, a practice that can lead to underachievement, lack of resilience, and inability to fail, recover, and work hard (Neihart et al, 2002; Peterson, 2003).

What effects does genetically modified corn have on the Monarch butterfly population (in conjunction with the life-cycle unit)? Why didn't Emily Dickinson publish any of her poetry (in conjunction with the poetry unit)? How did J.K. Rowling develop her characters in Harry Potter (in conjunction with a writing unit)? How did Krakatoa differ from Mount St. Helens (in conjunction with a geology unit)? Which countries still engage in whaling and what reasons do they have for doing so (in conjunction with study of endangered species)?

16 **Let students choose content.** This simple strategy builds ownership and, thus, quality into assignments and projects by students. Mrs. Wellman "let" students choose an animal on which to develop a report. They were studying oceans, and each student had to make a case concerning why he or she should be allowed to report on an animal they chose. In allowing choice in the content area of study and by having students explain why they should be allowed to have their chosen animal, she increased both interest and motivation prior to the assignment. One third grader was overheard explaining to her parents, "I got the Orca. Can you believe it? I get to do my ocean animal on the Orca. I can hardly wait to begin." Similarly, a Native American student, when given the opportunity to choose which president about whom to develop a biography, picked Andrew Jackson. He developed a biographical account of the influence of Jackson from the perspective of the Navajo people whom he had persecuted. This project was original, passionate, and resonated with the voice of the child who chose this president. Choice of content is a simple strategy that holds great potential for engaging students by putting them in charge of their projects and assignments.

17 **Offer students opportunities to choose products, audiences, and ways of presenting what they know.** Similar to allowing students choice of content, offering them choices concerning the types of products, the audiences with which they share their work, and how they share their work can be equally motivating to students. Roger, a student who in grade five had not yet learned to read, had been given a social studies assignment by his teacher. Fortunately for Roger, his teacher allowed students to show their understanding of the content in a variety of ways. His teacher posed three questions and asked the students to create something that demonstrated they understood the answers to the questions. Roger created a drawing in which he placed three sailing ships. He explained to his teacher that he "drew the ships chained together because they represented our three branches of government. None could sail in waters if the others would not let them." He further explained that "the banks of the river represented the United States constitution—the boundaries of the waters in which the ships could sail." Roger went on to point out the sails and "how the wind that blew them and moved the ships represented the will of the people who put the government into office." Finally, he described how "the river, in which the ships sailed, as it connected to the ocean represented the interconnectedness of our country with the rest of the world." Clearly, Roger understood. Yet, if he had been required to write answers to the three questions, his responses, due to his learning disability, would have revealed quite a different understanding than the one he conveyed using his art and metaphorical thinking. We do not intend to minimize the importance of reading and writing. Rather, we suggest that if teachers want to know whether students understand, then students ought to have a variety of ways available to them to express their understanding.

Likewise, students can participate in selecting outlets and audiences for their work. Students in an elementary school in Michigan created a poetry booklet, and through a simple brainstorming session concerning who should receive a copy of their publication, they thought well outside of the four walls of the classroom. They suggested that each child whose poem was published should receive a book as well as each classroom teacher and the school library. Students then thought they could donate one to the community library and some to doctor and dentist office waiting rooms in the community. Another student suggested that poems be displayed in local restaurants in the plastic "table tents" that restaurants usually use to advertise desserts and specials. (The restaurants provided free kids' meals to each child whose work they displayed.) Finally, some students suggested a grand opening at a local coffee shop in which their work would be read. Having an authentic audience helped to elevate the quality of their work. This work was made available for the community and interested audience members—a much more authentic audience than classroom teacher or parents. One teacher went so far as to create bulletin boards on which students kept track of all the different products and audiences that they created and touched during the school-year. The bulletin board then served as a menu of sorts for students who needed inspiration when choosing how to show what they learned.

18 Provide choice concerning whether to work alone or together.
Elementary schools today often seat children at tables and focus on group-work or cooperative learning. Group work provides students with the opportunity to learn collaborative skills and can also make school-work more enjoyable. But sometimes students view cooperative learning unfavorably, especially when group grades are attached, or when groups are assigned by ability levels without clear

roles in which each student can make a meaningful contribution (Kagan, 1993; Robinson, 1990). Some students would simply rather work alone. If the goal of the activity is to enhance students' collaborative skills, then group work is warranted. However, if the goal is for students to understand content, then teachers should consider students' learning preferences and offer them choices of whether to work alone or together. A student who would rather work alone and who does better work alone, should often have the option to work alone. In some classrooms these children are rarely given the option to work alone, and thus, they are denied a learning mode that best meets their educational needs.

When teachers seat students at tables, they force them to interact whether they work together or not. Sam picks on Sally, moves into her space, whispers put-downs, and quietly invades her thinking and learning space. Sally uses Suzie's stuff, and Suzie simply doesn't like Sally. The personality dynamics permeate the learning space, and behavior management becomes center-stage in the classroom as the teacher is forced to deal with tattling, spats, territorial battles, and stolen items. If students must be seated at tables, they need to have the option to go somewhere else to work, or as Mrs. Scanlon called it "set up an office" using a barrier of cardboard to provide privacy and space at the "table spot." After five years in school working at tables with other kids, one nine-year-old girl who would rather work alone wrote the following entry in her daily journal:

> If I could change one thing about my life it would be to have my own desk. If I had my own desk in school it would be great in lots of ways. I would have more room to move around. It would get me away from other students who tempt me to talk. I wouldn't have people putting their stuff in my space. Having my own space would give me room to concentrate without being bothered by Kevin. The best part would be having room for my items and my thinking. That is why I want my own desk.

19 **Offer students choices concerning due dates.** Providing students with choices for project due dates or order of presentations can not only help students learn self-regulation and time management, but it also offers them some control over their learning, which can lead to a sense of greater responsibility for their learning. For example, Mahera has soccer practice on Monday and Tuesday, with games every Saturday. If she had a project due on a Tuesday, it might be difficult for her to complete it. If she were allowed the opportunity to select the day to turn in her project, she might look at her schedule and choose a Friday, allowing herself more time to do a good job on the work.

Consider this example: Mrs. Lee assigned reports each quarter to her second and third graders with the same due date for all students. Then over the next several weeks she would have each student read his or her report. By the time some students had a turn to read, they had forgotten what they had written. Had she chosen to have two students each day bring and read their reports, some students would have continued to work on and polish their reports right up until the day they elected to present their finished work.

When a teacher creates a due date, then takes points for one day late and awards no points for two or more days late, smart underachievers know that they only need to wait until after the due date to avoid doing the assignment at all. Better to demand that they do the work, while at the same time ensuring that the work is worth doing. I have always viewed a due date like a pregnancy. It might be early, it might be on the due date, or it might be late, but it will happen. With this approach, students must do the work. Setting a window of time for them to turn in a large project and allowing them to choose the date during that window will lead to more projects turned in "on time." If students fail to finish by their due date, then it is their fault—not the teacher's fault—that their work isn't done. They own it.

20 Help students consider and evaluate the importance of their work by posing questions such as "So what?" "Who Cares?" "Who might care?" and "How might we have a greater effect?" These questions provide powerful opportunities for students and their teachers to consider whether what they are studying is important. If it seems unimportant (i.e., nobody would care about it and no one can figure out why someone would care about it), then consider spending less time on this content in favor of content that has greater meaning. Once determining that content is worth caring about, students and teachers can begin to consider what effects it might have on the classroom, school, community, or larger audience. For example, students in a small Michigan town wrote letters to the editor concerning a landfill in their community that had been proposed by an out-of-town developer. After sending their letters, they researched the wetlands protection act and attended township meetings. Their interest, knowledge of the situation, and tenacity resulted in denial of a permit for the landfill. These students learned about law, the environment, and how to affect change in their community by using communication and political action. Likewise, students in Kenosha,

Wisconsin, interviewed senior citizens and created a photo-journalistic display for the local history museum on the influence of immigration on Kenosha. In doing this project, students refined their written and oral communication skills, learned local history, and developed artistic displays that enriched their community.

21 **Connect school-work to the real world deliberately and often by engaging in community involvement, service-learning, mentorships, and apprenticeships.** Connecting students with the community and professionals in their areas of interest links them to our democracy and sets them up as future productive members of society. Schools often have as a goal to increase community involvement, and having community members to share their knowledge or work with interested students provides an authentic experience for the community members and students alike.

Trinity started a newspaper in his enrichment class and wrote columns about topics of local interests. His teacher sent one of his columns to the local paper, and the editor found his voice so fresh that she "hired" him to write a column a week. He was in the fifth grade at the time. Trinity continued to contribute to his local paper throughout middle school and high school, eventually as a paid employee. His journalism interests followed him to college!

Students in Victoria's school adopted a courtyard that they transformed into a bird and butterfly sanctuary. They worked with a local Department of Natural Resources officer and with a landscape architect in planning the courtyard. They used math, science, economics, and artistic design in this endeavor as they calculated how much mulch they needed, learned about which plants attracted which birds and butterflies and about the life cycles and needs of these animals, planned fund raising activities to help pay for the renovation, and designed the plantings and hardscape for the space. Eventually, they developed a courtyard brochure that described the specific flora and fauna they had brought to the school.

22 **Provide opportunities for deep involvement. Jacky came to school crazy about horses.** She read all of the Marguarite Henry and Walter Farley books in the library before fourth grade. Any assignment in which she was given a choice, she related to horses. She did reports on horse breeds, made a bridle rack in wood shop, drew horses in art, read horse books (both fiction and non fiction) in language arts, explained the geologic time eras through the evolution of Eohippus, and calculated the speed of muddy and dry tracks for both Standardbreds (trotters and pacers) and Thoroughbreds. She even did a language report on all the common sayings used in the English language that come from horses (e.g., don't look a gift horse in the mouth, getting a little long in the tooth, champing at the bit, rode hard and put up wet, you can lead a horse to water, but you can't make him drink). Rather than forbidding her to use horses in her educational projects, her teachers encouraged her to learn more about a topic that clearly excited her. One science teacher helped her learn genetics through studying the inherited patterns of coat colors, a concept that she found much more interesting than studying Mendel's peas. Her teachers helped her explore her passion about horses from a variety of angles. The amount of work and the quality of work that Jacky produced when she could connect it to horses was simply outstanding.

23 **Tell students to come see you if they have a better idea for an assignment, discussion . . . anything!** This strategy involves low creativity on the part of the teacher and the opportunity to be creative on the part of the student. As one second grader put it, "Teachers should ask the students because we often have great ideas about how to make school interesting." When giving students an assignment, simply offer them the option of "any other teacher-approved project." Students in a sixth-grade unit on simple machines found the lab activities both tedious and boring. They were not excited about dragging a weight up an inclined plane and calculating work, nor were they interested in how a pulley could reduce work. Their teacher was at her wits end. Student behavior was terrible, and their engagement was low. Finally, out of desperation she said to the students, "If someone has a better idea of how we might learn this unit I'd like to hear it." Two students suggested that it would be fun (and educational) if they could build complex machines out of the simple machines. Thus, a Rube Goldberg activity was implemented in this teacher's classroom. From this beginning, she offered students the chance to "improve" on her assignments, and often they suggested quality alternative activities. This approach not only allows for engagement and ownership by the students, but also provides the teacher with a variety of interesting and quality student responses to her content assignments. Just imagine what Jacky from strategy No. 22 might suggest related to horses and simple machines!

24 **Explicitly discuss process to encourage metacognition.** Understanding how students think, helping them to understand their own thinking, and recognizing that students think differently from each other provides a solid foundation for cognitive growth and student achievement. By talking with kids about how they solved a problem and helping them understand their thinking processes, we help them solve future problems. Did you write from an outline, or did you do the outline last? Neither is correct, and each reflects a particular style, one linear and the other holistic. Yet in some schools an outline is required, leaving the holistic learners thinking they write or think poorly. Leah came home at the beginning of her second-grade year distressed, explaining how the teacher was making her call a ten a one. She had been given the problem of adding 29 and 34. The teacher told her to add the nine and the four and carry the one. She asked why she would call it a one when it was really a ten. She would have solved the problem by adding 20 and 30 to get 50, then adding nine and four to get 13, then adding 50 and 13 to get 63. Renaming a ten as a one rightly confused her. There are many ways to understand and to solve problems, and if we are to develop a generation of students who can think, then we need to encourage thinking and thinking about thinking. The best way to do that is to discuss how and what is involved in thinking.

25 **Throw away the rubric and provide minimum requirements instead.** Rubrics are great tools for helping students understand what is expected of them. They provide guidelines concerning what is sub-standard, on-standard, and exemplary on a variety of criteria. Put simply, rubrics provide students (and their parents) recipes for successfully completing assignments and for earning high grades. Even at the university level, students seek rubrics so that they will know exactly what they have to do (and no more) to obtain an A on a project. We believe that rubrics should be used in moderation and on basic-skill types of assignments. If you want to know if a student can write a good paragraph, then provide an exemplar and criteria to guide that good paragraph. It is doubtful, however, that J. K. Rowling had a rubric for her Harry Potter books, or that Van Gogh had a rubric for his Starry Night painting.

If the assignment is important, then provide students with a floor of minimum requirements, rather than with a ceiling of exemplars. By providing exemplary criteria, we tell the students what is exemplary before they ever begin to engage in thinking about how they might develop a high-quality response to our assignment. In short, they follow our recipe. Rarely, do they go beyond what we have already defined as exemplary. In effect, we put a lid on the assignment before the students ever begin work. It is like the difference between a cook who follows a recipe and a chief who creates the recipe. If we want to develop students who can think, solve problems, define problems, and who are capable of original thought, then we need to encourage such actions on a regular basis.

By providing them with minimum criteria, we provide students with a starting place. They know what has to be done to earn a C. They can then decide whether they want to exceed the minimum and apply themselves to define and develop an exemplary response to the task. If they choose the C, don't criticize their choice. Perhaps they don't view the assignment as particularly interesting or important, or perhaps they have other priorities. Whatever the case, they are learning to make decisions about their learning and we should support this developing autonomy. Many students will, however, seek an A. Some will be upset and demand to know exactly what is required for an A. A good answer to such queries is "more than the minimum requirements," or "what will it take for you to develop an exemplary project?" Both responses will frustrate and challenge the students, a first step to engaging them in generating quality work in response to the assignment.

The simple machine unit that we discussed in Strategy No. 23 involved using minimum criteria. The teachers simply told the students that they "had to build it, demonstrate it, and that they had to use and be able to identify at least three simple machines." For the final minimum criteria the teacher explained that "each machine had to have a purpose and do something." If students met these minimum criteria, they would earn the grade of C. This ambiguity drove the A-getting, teacher-pleasing students crazy. How could their teacher be so vague? When they demanded more structure, their teacher smiled and encouraged them to apply themselves to the task, to prove to her that they could produce creative, exemplary work. Basically, she set no limits and the students responded by producing excellent and different machines. The variety and originality in their responses provided interest, learning, and enjoyment to their peers and to their teachers. These results are the antithesis of 25 very similar projects developed in response to a common rubric.

One student, Megan, built a toothpaste dispenser out of a series of levers and inclined planes with a pulley for good measure, but when the hammer dispensed the toothpaste, it did so with such force that it shot the toothpaste to the classroom wall. The students that year had agreed that to earn an A the machine must also "work." After the toothpaste hit the wall, a heated discussion ensued concerning whether or not the machine had worked. The naysayers argued that the toothpaste should have been dispensed onto the toothbrush, whereas the supporters said that the machine had after all dispensed the toothpaste. In the middle of the fray, Megan simply took the toothbrush out of the machine and taped it to the wall. Problem solved—creatively. Students in this teacher's class began to ask for more open-ended criteria in their assignments and less structure as they became comfortable with their creative selves.

As you begin to put the students in charge of their learning using this menu of strategies, you encourage creativity, autonomy, buy-in, interest, quality, strengths, and the development of student talent. These strategies often require less teacher-work and more student thinking and involvement, leaving teachers more energized at the end of the day. One day, maybe it will be "cool to be smart" and maybe the students will learn for the sake of learning—because they care and because learning is fun. Until that day comes, we need to gently show them the way and develop an environment of achievement. It is our hope that these strategies can provide teachers with some positive steps in that direction—toward making the mission of school discussed at this chapter's beginning come alive.

REFERENCES

Amrein, A. L., & Berliner, D. C. (2002). *An analysis of some unintended and negative consequences of high-stakes testing.* Tempe: Arizona State University, Educational Policy Studies Laboratory. (EPSL No. 0211-125-EPRU)

Bandura, A. (1994). Self-efficacy. In V. S. Ramachaudran (Ed.), *Encyclopedia of human behavior* (Vol. 4, pp. 71-81). New York: Academic Press.

Bloom. B. S. (1985). *Developing talent in young people.* New York: Ballantine Books.

Brown, S. B., Archambault, F. X., Zhang, W., & Westberg, K. (1994, April). *The impact of gifted students on the classroom practices of teachers.* Paper presented at the annual conference of the Amcrican Educational Research Association, New Orleans, LA.

Brulles, D. (2005). An examination and critical analysis of cluster grouping giftcd students in an elementary school. (Unpublished doctoral dissertation, Arizona State University).

Bryant, M. A. (1987). Meeting the needs of gifted first grade children in a heterogeneous classroom. *Roeper Review, 9* , 214-216.

Burns, M. (2000). *About teaching mathematics : A K-8 resource* (2nd ed.). Sausalito, Calif.: Math Solutions Publications.

Colangelo, N, Assouline, S. G., & Gross, M. U. M, (2004). *A nation deceived: How schools hold back America's brightest students* (Vol 2). Iowa City, IA: University of Iowa.

Coleman, M. R. (1995). The importance of cluster grouping. *Gifted Child Today, 18*(1), 38-40.

Coleman, L. J., & Cross, T. L. (2005). *Being gifted in school: An introduction to development, guidance, and teaching (*2nd ed.*)*. Waco, TX: Prufrock Press, Inc.

Csikszentmihalyi, M., Rathunde, K. & Whalen, S. (1997). *Talented teenagers: The roots of success and failure*. New York: Cambridge University Press.

Davis, G. A., & Rimm, S. W. (2004). *Education of the gifted and talented (5th ed.)*. Englewood Cliffs, NJ: Prentice-Hall.

Delcourt, M. A. B., & Evans, K. (1994). *Qualitative extension of the learning outcomes study*. Storrs, CT: The National Research Center on the Gifted and Talented.

Delcourt, M. A. B., Loyd, B. H., Cornell, D. G., & Goldberg, M.D. (1994). *Evaluation of the effects of programming arrangements on student learning outcomes*. Storrs, CT: The National Research Center on the Gifted and Talented.

Dewey, J. (1916). *Democracy and education*. New York: McMillan.

Eide, B., & Eide, F. (2006). *The mislabeled child*. New York: Hyperion.

Eisner, E. (2001). *What does it mean to say a school is doing well?* Phi Delta Kappan, 82(5), 367-372.

Fulan, M., & Campbell, C. (2006). *Unlocking the potential for district-wide reform*. The Literacy and Numeracy Secretariat, Ministry of Education, Ontario, Canada.

Gall, M. (1970). The use of questions in teaching. *Review of Educational Research, 40*(5), pp. 07-721

Gates, J. C. (2007). ADHD and/or gifted: The possibility for misdiagnosis. Paper presented at the World Council for Gifted and Talented Children, 17th Biennial World Conference England: Warwick.

Gentry, M. (1999). *Promoting student achievement and exemplary classroom practices through cluster grouping: A research-based alternative to heterogeneous elementary classrooms* (Research Monograph 99138). Storrs, CT: University of Connecticut, National Research Center on the Gifted and Talented.

Gentry, M. & Hu, S., & Thomas, A. T. (in press). Race and ethnicity in gifted education. In C. M. Callahan & J. A. Plucker (Eds.), *Critical issues and practices in gifted education: What research says* (pp.195-212). Waco, Texas: Prufrock Press

Gentry, M. & Hu, S., & Thomas, A. T. (2008). Ethnically diverse students. In J. Plucker & C. Callahan (Eds), *Critical issues and practices in gifted education* (pp.195-212). Waco, TX: Prufrock Press, Inc.

Gentry, M. & Keilty, W. (2004). On-going staff development planning and implementation: Keys to program success. *Roeper Review, 26*, 148-156.

Gentry, M. & Owen, S. V. (1999). An investigation of total school flexible cluster grouping on identification, achievement, and classroom practices. *Gifted Child Quarterly, 43*, 224-243.

George, P. (1995). Is it possible to live with tracking and ability grouping? In H. Pool & J. A. Page, (Eds.), *Beyond tracking: Finding success in inclusive schools.* Bloomington Indiana: Phi Delta Kappan Educational Foundation.

Graesser, A. C., & Person, N. K. (1994). Question asking during tutoring. *American Educational Research Journal, 31*(1), 104-137.

Gubbins, E. J., Westberg, K. L., Reis, S. M., Dinnocenti, S., Tieso, C. M., Muller, L. M., Park, S., Emerick, L. J., Maxfield, L. R., & Burns, D.E. (2002). *Implementing a professional development model using gifted education strategies with all students* (RM02172). Storrs, CT: The National Research Center on the Gifted and Talented, University of Connecticut.

Hestenes, L. L., Cassidy, D. J., & Niemeyer, J. (2004). A microanalysis of teachers' verbalizations in inclusive classrooms. *Early Education and Development, 15* (1), p. 23-38.

Hieronymus, A. N., Hoover, H. D., & Lindquist, E. F. (1984). *Iowa tests of basic skills* (Form G). Chicago: Riverside Publishing Company.

Hoover, S., Sayler, M., & Feldhusen, J. F. (1993). Cluster grouping of elementary students at the elementary level. *Roeper Review, 16*, 13-15.

Ivey, J. D. (1965). Computation skills: Results of acceleration. *The Arithmetic Teacher, 12*, 39-42.

Kagan, S. (1992). *Cooperative learning.* San Clemente, CA: Kagan Publishing.

Kaplan, S. (In press). In J. S. Renzulli, E. J. Gubbins, K. S. McMillen, R. D. Eckert, & C. A. Little (Eds.), *Systems and models for developing programs for the gifted and talented.* Mansfield Center, CT: Creative Learning Press.

Kaplan, S. & Cannon, M. W. (2001). *Curriculum starter cards: Developing differentiated lessons for gifted students.* Waco, TX: Prufrock Press.

Kennedy, D. M. (1989). Classroom interactions of gifted and non gifted fifth graders. Unpublished doctoral dissertation, Purdue University, West Lafayette, IN.

Kennedy, D. M. (1995). Teaching gifted in regular classrooms: Plain talk about creating a gifted-friendly classroom. *Roeper Review, 17*, 232-234.

Kettle, K. E., Renzulli, J. S., & Rizza, M. G. (1998). Exploring student preferences for product development: My way . . . An expression style instrument. *Gifted Child Quarterly, 42* (1), 49-60.

Kloss, R. J., (1988.) Toward asking the right questions: The beautiful, the pretty, and the big messy ones. *The Clearing House, 61*, 245-248.

Kulik, J. A. (1992). *An analysis of the research on ability grouping: Historical and contemporary perspectives.* Storrs, CT: The National Research Center on the Gifted and Talented.

Kulik, J. A. (2003). Grouping and tracking. In N. Colangelo & G. Davis (Eds.) *Handbook of gifted education* (pp. 268-281). Boston: Allyn & Bacon.

Kulik, C.-L. C., & Kulik, J. A. (1984). Effects of ability grouping on elementary school pupils: A meta-analysis. Paper presented at the annual meeting of the American Psychological Association, Toronto. (ERIC Document Reproduction Service No. ED 255 329)

Kulik, C.-L. C., & Kulik J. A. (1985). Effects of ability grouping on achievement and self-esteem. Paper presented at the annual convention of the American Psychological Association, Los Angeles, CA.

Kulik, J. A., & Kulik, C.-L. C. (1992). Meta-analytic findings on grouping programs. *Gifted Child Quarterly, 36,* 73-77.

Kulik, J. A., & Kulik, C.-L. C. (1991). Ability grouping and gifted students. In N. Colangelo & G.A. Davis (Eds.), *Handbook of gifted education* (pp. 178-196). Boston: Allyn and Bacon.

LaRose, B. (1986). The lighthouse program: A longitudinal research project. *Journal for the Education of the Gifted, 9,* 224-32.

Lewis, B. (1998). *Kid's guide to social action: How to solve the social problems you choose and turn creative thinking into positive action.* Minneapolis, MN: Free Spirit Press.

Long, R. G. (1957). A comparative study of the effects of an enriched program for the talented in advanced algebra classes. *Dissertation Abstracts International, 18,* 529. (University Microfilms No. 00-24831)

Lou, Y., Abrami, P. C., Spence, J. C., Poulsen, C., Chambers, B., & d'Apollonia, S. (1996). Within-class grouping: A meta analysis. *Review of Educational Research, 66*(4), 423-458.

Mann, R. L. (n.d.). Me, myself, and I. Unpublished document.

Marsh, H. W., Chessor, D., Craven, R., & Roche, L. (1995). The effects of gifted and talented programs on academic self-concept: The big fish strikes again. *American Educational Research Journal, 32*, 285-319.

McBrien, J. L., & Brandt, R. S. (1997). *The language of learning: A guide to education terms.* Alexandria, VA: Association for Supervision and Curriculum Development.

Miller, L. S. (2004). Promoting sustained growth in the representation of African Americans, Latinos, and Native Americans among top students in the United States at all levels of the education system (RM04190). Storrs, CT: National Research Center on the Gifted and Talented.

Mills, S. R., Rice, C. T., Berliner, D. C., & Rousseau, E. W. (1980). The correspondence between teacher questions and student answers in classroom discourse. *Journal of Experimental Education, 48*(3), 194-209.

Moon, S. M. (2004). Using the Purdue three-stage model to develop talent in science and technology. In S. Cho, H. Seo, & J. Lee (Eds.), *Rebirth of Giftedness in the Trans-Modern Society: Vision, Values, and Leadership.* Proceedings of the 8th Asia-Pacific Conference on Giftedness (pp. 66-74). Daejeon, Korea: The Asia-Pacific Federation of the World Council for Gifted Children.

Moon, S.M. (2003). Personal Talent. *High Ability Studies, 14*(1), 5-21.

Moon, S. M., Kolloff, M. B., Robinson, A., Dixon, F., & Feldhusen, J. F. (In press). The Purdue three-stage model. In J. S. Renzulli & J. Gubbins (Eds.), *Systems and models for developing programs for the gifted and talented.* Mansfield Center, CT: Creative Learning Press.

Oakes, J. (1985). *Keeping track: How schools structure inequality.* New Haven, CT: Yale University Press.

Neihart, M., Reis, S., Robinson, N., & Moon, S. (Eds.) (2002). *The social and emotional development of gifted children: What do we know?* Waco, TX: Prufrock Press.

Peterson, J. S. (2003). An argument for proactive attention to affective concerns of gifted adolescents. *Journal of Secondary Gifted Education, 14*(2), 62-71.

Peterson, J. S., & Ray, K. E. (2006a). Bullying and the gifted: Victims, perpetrators, prevalence, and effects. *Gifted Child Quarterly,* 50, 148-168.

Peterson, J. S., & Ray, K. E. (2006b). Bullying among the gifted: The subjective experience. *Gifted Child Quarterly,* 50, 252-269.

Pierce, R. L., Cassady, J. C., Adams, C. M., Dixon, F. D., Speirs Neumeister, K. L., & Cross, T. L. (2007, April). Cluster grouping and the academic achievement of gifted students. Paper presented at the Annual Convention of the American Educational Research Association, Chicago, IL.

Phenix, P. (1964). *Realms of meaning.* New York: McGraw-Hill.

Purcell, J. (1994). *The status of programs for high-ability students* (CRS94306). Storrs, CT: University of Connecticut, The National Research Center on the Gifted and Talented.

Purcell, J. H., & Renzulli, J. S. (1998). *Total talent portfolio: A systematic plan to identify and nurture gifts and talents.* Mansfield Center, CT: Creative Learning Press.

Reis, S. M., Burns, D. E., & Renzulli, J. S. (1992). *Curriculum compacting: The complete guide to modifying the regular curriculum for high-ability students.* Mansfield Center, CT: Creative Learning Press.

Reis, S. M., Gentry, M., & Park, S. (1995). *Extending the pedagogy of gifted education to all students: The enrichment cluster study.* Technical Report. Storrs, CT: The National Research Center on the Gifted and Talented.

Renzulli, J. S. (1977). *Enrichment triad model: A guide for developing defensible programs for gifted and talented.* Mansfield, CT: Creative Learning Press.

Renzulli, J. S. (1978). What makes giftedness? Reexamining a definition. *Phi Delta Kappan, 60*(3), 180-184, 261.

Renzulli, J. S. (1982). What makes a problem real: Stalking the illusive meaning of qualitative differences in gifted education. *Gifted Child Quarterly, 26*(4), 147-156.

Renzulli, J. S. (Ed.) (1986). *Systems and models for developing programs for the gifted and talented.* Mansfield Center, CT: Creative Learning Press.

Renzulli, J. S. (1994). *Schools for talent development: A comprehensive plan for total school improvement.* Mansfield Center, CT: Creative Learning Press.

Renzulli, J. S. (2002). Emerging conceptions of giftedness: Building a bridge to the new century. *Exceptionality, 10*(2), 67-75.

Renzulli, J. S. (2005, May). A quiet crisis is clouding the future of R & D. *Education Week, 24*(38), 32-33. 40.

Renzulli, J. S., Gentry, M., & Reis, S. M. (2003). *Enrichment clusters: A practical plan for real-world, student-driven learning.* Mansfield Center, CT: Creative Learning Press.

Renzulli, J., Leppien, J., & Hays, T. (2000). *The multiple menu model: A critical guide for developing differentiated curriculum.* Mansfield Center, CT: Creative Learning Press.

Renzulli, J. S., & Reis, S. M. (1991). The reform movement and the quiet crisis in gifted education. *Gifted Child Quarterly, 35*, 26-35.

Renzulli, J. S., & Reis, S. M. (1994). Research related to the Schoolwide Enrichment Triad model. *Gifted Child Quarterly, 38*(1), 7-20.

Renzulli, J. S., & Reis, S. M. (1997). *The schoolwide enrichment model: A comprehensive plan for educational excellence* (2nd ed.). Mansfield Center, CT: Creative Learning Press.

Renzulli, J. S., Smith, L. H., White, A. J., Callahan, C. M., Hartman, R. K., & Westberg, K. L. (2002). *Scales for rating the behavioral characteristics of superior students*. Mansfield Center, CT: Creative Learning Press.

Rimm-Kaufman, S. E., & Sawyer, B. E. (2004). Primary-grade teachers' self-efficacy beliefs, attitudes toward teaching, and discipline and teaching practice priorities in relation to the Responsive Classroom approach. *Elementary School Journal,* 104, 321-341.

Robert, J. L. & Inman, T. F. (2007). *Differentiating instruction: Best practices for the classroom*. Waco, TX: Prufrock Press.

Robinson, A. (1990). Cooperation or exploitation? The argument against cooperative learning for talented students. *Journal for the Education of the Gifted, 4*(3), 9-23.

Robinson, N. M., Reis, S. M., Neihart, M., & Moon, S. M. (2002). Social and emotional issues facing gifted and talented students: What have we learned and what should we do now? In M. Neihart, S. M. Reis, N. M. Robinson & S. M. Moon (Eds.), *The social and emotional development of gifted children: What do we know?* (pp. 267-289). Waco, TX: Prufrock Press.

Rogers, K. B. (1991). *The relationship of grouping practices to the education of the gifted and talented learner.* Storrs, CT: University of Connecticut, The National Research Center on the Gifted and Talented.

Rogers, K. B. (1993). Grouping the gifted and talented: Questions and answers. *Roeper Review, 16*, 8-12.

Rogers, K. B. (2002). *Re-forming gifted education*. Scottsdale, AZ: Great Potential Press.

Schuler, P. A. (1998). *Cluster grouping coast to coast.* Storrs, CT: The National Research on the Gifted and Talented. (Research Report 1998-00-00)

Senge, P. (1991). *The fifth discipline: The art and discipline of the learning organization*. New York: Doubleday.

Slavin, R. E. (1990) Ability grouping and student achievement in elementary schools: A best-evidence synthesis. *Review of Educational Research, 57*, 293-336.

Slavin, R. E. (1987a). Ability grouping: A best-evidence synthesis. *Review of Educational Research, 57*, 293-336.

Slavin, R. E. (1987b). Grouping for instruction. *Equity and Excellence, 23*(1, 2), 31-36.

Slavin, R. E. (2006). *Educational psychology: Theory and practice.* Boston: Pearson.

State of the States (2007). *State of the states*. Washington, D.C.: National Association for Gifted Children, author.

Teno, K. M. (2000). Cluster grouping elementary gifted students in the regular classroom: A teacher's perspective. *Gifted Child Today, 23*, 44-49.

Tieso, C. L. (2003). Ability grouping is not just tracking anymore. *Roeper Review, 26*, 29-36.

Tieso, C. L. (2005). The effects of grouping practices and curricular adjustments on achievement. *Journal for the Education of the Gifted, 29*, 60-89.

Tomlinson, C. (1995). Deciding to differentiate instruction in middle school: One school's journey. *Gifted Child Quarterly, 3*(9), 77-87.

Tomlinson, C. (1999). *The differentiated classroom: Responding to the needs of all learners.* Alexandria, VA: Association for Supervision and Curriculum Development.

Tomlinson, C. (2001). *How to differentiate instruction in mixed-ability classrooms* (2nd ed.). Alexandria, VA: Association for Supervision and Curriculum Development.

Tomlinson, C. A., & Callahan, C. M. (1992). Contributions of gifted education to general education in a time of change. *Gifted Child Quarterly, 36,* 183-189.

United States Department of Education. (1993). *National excellence: A case for developing America's talent.* Washington, DC: United States Government Printing Office

United States Department of Education (2000). OCR Elementary and Secondary School Survey: 2000. Retrieved February 1, 2006, from http://vistademo. beyond2020.com/ocr2000r

Van Deur, P. (2003). Gifted primary students' knowledge of self directed learning. *International Education Journal, 4*(4), 64 - 74.

VanTassel-Baska, J. (2003). What matters in curriculum for gifted learners: Reflections on theory, research, and practice. In N. Colangelo & G. A. Davis (Eds.), *Handbook of gifted education* (3rd ed., pp. 174-183). Boston: Allyn & Bacon.

Vygotsky, L. S. (1978). *Mind in society: The development of higher psychological processes.* Cambridge, MA: Harvard University Press.

Ward, V. (1981). Basic concepts. In W. B. Barbe & J. S. Renzulli, *Psychology and education of the gifted* (3rd ed., pp. 66-76). New York: Irvington.

Webb, J. T. (2000). Misdiagnosis and dual diagnosis of gifted children. In M. Neihart (Ed.), *Symposium on cutting edge minds: What it means to be exceptional*. Scottsdale, AZ: Great Potential Press.

Webb, J. T., Amend, E. R., Webb, N. E., Goerss, J., Beljan, P., & Olenchak, F. R. (2005). *Misdiagnosis and dual diagnoses of gifted children and adults: ADHD, bipolar, OCD, asperger's, depression, and other disorders.* Scottsdale, AZ: Great Potential Press.

Wormeli, R. (2006). *Fair isn't always equal: Assessing and grading in the differentiated classroom*. Westerville, OH: Stenhouse Publishers.

Ziehl, D. C. (1962). An evaluation of an elementary school enriched instructional program. Dissertation Abstracts International, 24, 2743. (University Microfilms No. 6204644)

A

INSTRUMENTS, FORMS & CHECKLISTS

Student Data Summary Card

School Year:

Name:

Gender: M   F   Race:

Current Grade: Projected Grade:

	Language Arts	Math	Science
State Test			
NWEA			

Final Reading Grade:

Final Math Grade:

Running Record A-Z:

Identification Category (circle one):   High Achieving   Above Average   Average   Low Average   Low

Special Education (achievement level):

English Proficiency Level: 1   2   3   4   5   N/A

Discipline Issues: Never   Seldom   Often

Attendance Issues: Never   Seldom   Often

Other Comments:

APPLICATION FOR TEACHER OF HIGH ACHIEVEMENT STUDENT GROUP

Name: _____

Detail your experience working with high-achieving students.

_____
_____
_____
_____
_____

List relevant education and background in working with high-achieving students (include course-work, workshops, conferences, degrees, certifications etc).

_____
_____
_____
_____
_____

List grade levels you are willing to teach.   K   1   2   3   4   5   6

Are you willing to wait 3 years for this appointment?   Yes   No

If yes, during the time before the appointment, what actions would you take to increase your knowledge in this area?

_____
_____
_____
_____

Explain why teaching this group of students interests you.

_____
_____
_____

Me, Myself, and I!

A Total Talent Portfolio

_____   _____   _____
     My Name   My Teacher's Name   My Grade

This booklet is about you! This interest inventory asks you to answer a series of questions about subjects you like best in school and activities you prefer to do outside of school. The answers to the questions should be your answers, not your friend's or your neighbor's answers. The reason we are asking you to complete this inventory is so we can get to know you better. If we know what fascinates you and how you like to learn best, we can help make your days in school more interesting and successful.

Thank you and have fun!

"Kids" graphic by David Jernigan

School Subjects

Circle the smiley face that shows best how you feel about each of the subjects listed below.

Subject	Feeling
Art	☺——😐——☹
Geography	☺——😐——☹
Gym	☺——😐——☹
Math	☺——😐——☹
Music	☺——😐——☹
Reading	☺——😐——☹
Science	☺——😐——☹
Social Studies	☺——😐——☹
Writing	☺——😐——☹

Interests

Use numbers to rank the areas below. Put a 1 next to your favorite activity, a 2 next to your second favorite, etc.

Interest	Rank
Acting	
Arts & Crafts	
Cartooning	
Creative Writing	
Community Service	
Dancing	
Geography	
History	
Music	
Science Experiments	
Technology/Computers	
Other	

List some topics you would love to learn more about:

_____

_____

_____

_____

Learning Style

People like to learn in very different ways. Some people like to read to find out new information. Some people like to put something together to figure it out. Think about how your like to learn new materials. Do you like it when people tell you something? Do you like to watch someone do something first? Use numbers to rank the areas below. Put a 1 next to the way you like to learn best, a 2 next to the way you like to learn second best, etc.

Learning Style	Rank
Computer Activities 📄	
Experiments (trial & error) ✗✔	
Speakers 👪	
CDs &Tapes 💿	
Learning Games ⬛	
Putting Things Together ⚒	
Reading 📚	
Watching Other People 👁	
Watching Videos 📹	

Sharing Style

After learning something new, it is wonderful to be able to share it with other people. What ways do you like to share new information? Circle the smiley face that shows best how you feel when you are asked to share in the ways listed below.

Style	Feeling		
Act or role play	☺	😐	☹
Make a display or model	☺	😐	☹
Draw a picture or a diagram	☺	😐	☹
Explain or discuss	☺	😐	☹
Take a test	☺	😐	☹
Do a worksheet	☺	😐	☹
Write a report	☺	😐	☹
Any other ideas?			

Short Term Goal

During the next year, I would like to:

_____

Environment

Some like it hot! Some like it bright! Which one is just right?

How do you like the room to be when you are trying to learn something? Make a mark on the lines below where you like it best.

Noise:

Very Quiet Mostly Quiet A little noise is OK Quite a bit of noise is OK Very Noisy

Light:

Dark Dim Light but not too bright Nice and light Very Bright

Temperature:

Cold Cool Mild Mild Hot

Working with Others

Some people like to work alone, and some people like to work with others. How about you? Circle the smiley face that best describes you.

I like to work alone. ☺ 😐 ☹	I like to work with one other child. ☺ 😐 ☹
I like to work with an adult. ☺ 😐 ☹	I like to work with a small group of friends. ☺ 😐 ☹
I like to work with a whole class. ☺ 😐 ☹	

These are the activities I do and lessons I take outside of school:

_____

_____

_____

_____

When I have free time at home, this is what I like to do:

_____

_____

_____

_____

Special family activities and experiences are:

_____

During your daydreaming time, what do you imagine you will be when you grow up? Draw a picture of yourself in the future!

Parents, now it's your turn!

Please complete this section to help us get a better picture of your child.

List four words that describe your child.

After school and on weekends my child,

_____

_____

_____

_____

_____

_____

_____

_____

I feel my child's best subject is

I feel my child's most difficult subject is

_____

_____

My child likes to collect

My child's favorite toys is

_____

_____

My child's favorite book is

My child's favorite TV program is

_____

_____

My child's favorite sport is

My child's favorite game is

_____

_____

Place an X on the line below to complete the following sentence. My child prefers to spend

Alone	With a few friends	Surrounded by people

I anticipate that my child will need guidance this year in the following area (reading, organization, peer relations):

_____

In the past, the following teaching techniques or types of activities have helped my child to be successful in school:

_____

My goal(s) for my child this year in school is (are):

_____

My long term goal(s) for my child is (are):

_____

"Kids" graphic by David Jernigan

Product Planning Guide

Artistic Products			
Architecture	Batik	Landscaping	Puzzles
Murals	Exhibits	Terrariums	Car designs
Decoration	Cartoons	Mosaic	Maps
Sculpture	Book covers/designs	Collage	Sewing
Filmstrips	Fabric design	Silk screens	Puppets
Slide shows	Maps	Movies	Set design
Comic strips	Mobiles	Videos	Tin ware
Yearbook	Fashion design	Aquariums	Pottery
Advertisements	Jewelry	Painting	Iron work
Drawing	Diorama	Web pages	Weaving
Graphic design	Furniture design	Package design	Calligraphy
Photography	Wood carvings	Postcards	Tessellations
Engraving	Political cartoons	Posters	Multimedia presentations
Etching	Horticultural design	Computer graphics	

Performance Products			
Skits	Dance	Films/videos	Interpretive song
Role playing	Mime	Reader's theater	Composition
Simulations	Puppet shows	Poetry readings	Chorale
Theatrical performance	Dramatic monologues	Improvisations	Concerts
Vocal	Comic performances	Musical performance	Parades
Athletic events	Demonstrations	Experiments	Reenactments

Spoken Products			
Debates	Lecture	D. J. shows	Book talks
Speeches	Mock trials	Panel discussions	Chronicles
Radio plays	Songs	Celebrity roasts	Forums
Advertisements	Sales promotions	Narrations	Sign language
Poetry readings	Simulations	Sermons	Puppet shows
Storytelling	Demonstrations	Dedication ceremonies	Book reviews
Poetry for two voices	Phone conversations	Weather reports	Audiotapes
Interviews	Eulogies	Rap songs	Infomercials
Oral histories	Announcements	Town crier	Master of ceremony
Newscasts	Comedy routines	Guided tours	Oral reports

Visual Products			
Videos	Layouts	Ice sculptures	Maps
Slide/digital photo shows	Models	Demonstrations	Diagrams
Computer printouts	Pottery	Cartoons	Mobiles
Sculptures	Proclamations	Travel brochures	Set design
Table settings	Computer programs	Athletic skills	Experiments
Advertisements	Timelines	Blueprints	Caricatures
Puppets	Diagrams/charts	Lists	Silk screening
Calendars	Sketches	Multimedia presentations	Graphic organizer
Musical scores	Graphs	Graphic design	Photography
Book jackets	Collages	Paintings	Fashion design

Product Planning Guide

Models/Construction Products

Drama sets	Gardens	Bird houses	Instruments
Sculpture	Dioramas	Bulletin boards	Robots
Relief map	Shelters	Circuit boards	Machines
Habitat	Collections	Paper engineering	Rockets
Bridges	Ceremonies	Puppet theaters	Play facilities
Inventions	Learning centers	Computer programs	Quilts
Food	Pottery	Computers	Multimedia presentation
Vehicles	Working models	Documentaries	Hydroponic farms
Fitness trails	Ant farms	Exhibitions	Masks
Microscopes	Buildings	Interviews	Robots
Microscope slides	Toys	Scale models	Gifts
Aqueducts	Games	3-D figures	Catalogs
Terrariums	Books	Graphs	Mazes
Greenhouses	Solar collectors	Furniture	Blueprints

Leadership Products

Speeches	Mock trails	Open forums	Service learning projects
Plans	Musical performances	Fund raising	Editing a newspaper
School patrols	Elections	Student council/government	Directing a plan
Leading rallies	Debates	Organizing a business	Discussion group on Internet
Consensus building	Campaigns	Organizing a group	Club or class webmaster
Role playing	Protests	Editorials	

Written Products

Pamphlets	Parables	Analyses	Budgets
Brochures	Advertisements	Epics	Criteria listings
Books	Laws	Web pages	Census reports
Speeches	Graphs	Autobiographies	Folktales
Captions	Notes	Flow charts	Graphic organizers
Charts	Diaries/journals	Amendments	Story problems
Radio programs	Poetry	Family trees	Public service announcements
Instructions	Marketing plans	Position statements	Ethnography
Interview questions	Comic strips	Banners	Maps
Outlines	Jokes/riddles	Plays/skits	Timelines
Simulations	Slogans	Letters/postcards	Multimedia presentations
Recipes	Songs/lyrics	Crossword puzzles	Discussion group questions
Legends	Questionnaires	Summaries	Limericks
Definitions	Invitations	Consumer reports	Grants
Bibliographies	Storyboards	Lists	
Rhymes	Greeting cards	Articles (newspaper, journal, etc.)	

Adapted from Renzulli, J. S., Leppien, J. H., & Hays, T. S. (2000). *The multiple menu model.* Mansfield Center, CT: Creative Learning Press.

INDIVIDUAL EDUCATIONAL PROGRAMMING GUIDE
The Compactor

Prepared by: Joseph S. Renzulli
Linda M. Smith

NAME _____

SCHOOL _____

AGE _____ TEACHER(S) _____

GRADE _____ PARENT(S) _____

Individual Conference Dates And Persons
Participating in Planning Of IEP

_____

CURRICULUM AREAS TO BE CONSIDERED FOR COMPACTING Provide a brief description of basic material to be covered during this marking period and the assessment information or evidence that suggests the need for compacting.	PROCEDURES FOR COMPACTING BASIC MATERIAL Describe activities that will be used to guarantee proficiency n basic curricular areas.	ACCELERATION AND/OR ENRICHMENT ACTIVITIES Describe activities that will be used to provide advanced level learning experiences in each area of the regular curriculum.

☐ Check here if additional information is recorded on the reverse side.

INDEPENDENT STUDY PLAN

Name _____

Teacher _____

Beginning Date _____

Estimated Ending Date _____

General Areas of Study (check all that apply)

Science	Language Arts	Social Studies	Art
Math	Music	Other	

What is the topic of your study?

_____

_____

What do you hope to find out?

_____

_____

List three things you will do to get started.

1. _____

2. _____

3. _____

Teacher Verification Section: Student has completed above three tasks.

_____
(teacher signature)

List the resources you will use during your study (books, Internet sites, magazines, videos, maps, people, etc.)

_____

_____

_____

What form will your final product take?

_____

_____

With whom will you share your product?

_____

INDEPENDENT STUDY LOG

Name

Teacher

Date

Project Title

My three goals:

1.

2.

3.

Reflection:

Did I accomplish my goals?

What did I do well?

_____

_____

_____

What could I have done better?

_____

_____

_____

_____

Next week I will . . . (Record three goals for the next week on your next log sheet.)

_____

_____

_____

_____

Independent Study Presentation Form
I AM READY TO PRESENT!

Name _____

Teacher _____

Date _____

Project Title _____

I would like to present my project to the following classes or groups:

_____

_____

_____

The length of my presentation is approximately _____

I will require the following equipment:

_____

_____

_____

I need to remember to take the following papers and materials with me:

_____

_____

_____

_____

The best time of day for me to present my project is:

_____

_____

INDEPENDENT STUDY STUDENT EVALUATION

Name _____

Teacher _____

Topic of Study _____

Project Title _____

What do you think was the best part of your independent study?

_____

_____

_____

Now that you have more experience, what are some things you would do better or differently?

_____

_____

_____

What are some questions that you still have about your topic?

_____

_____

_____

What suggestions would you have for another student who is interested in doing an independent study?

_____

_____

_____

STRATEGIES FOR ENSURING CHALLENGE

Strategy	Frequency of Use			
	Consistently	Often	Occasionally	Never
1. Introduce new concepts				
2. Present advanced content and consult advanced resources				
3. Develop products and services				
4. Use authentic methods and tools				
5. Use advanced vocabulary				
6. Integrate creative thinking				
7. Consider historical perspectives				
8. Engage students in presentations and performances				
9. Respond to student interests				
10. Encourage student-directed learning and choice				
11. Focus on problem solving, critical and creative thinking				
12. Provide curricular extensions and enrichments				
13. Use open-ended questions and activities				
14. Implement curriculum compacting and give credit to students who meet standards				
15. Adjust assignments based on student's skill level				
16. Provide many choices				

No.	Item				
17.	Accelerate students				
18	Offer independent study by providing time to become involved in long-term study in an area of passion				
19.	Provide opportunities for mentorships, apprentice-ships, community service, and service learning				
20.	Encourage positive affective development and self-evaluation				
21.	Hold high expectations for quality work				

B

HIGH-QUALITY DIFFERENTIATION RESOURCES

HIGH-QUALITY DIFFERENTIATION RESOURCES
A GUIDE TO A BASIC LIBRARY OF RESOURCES

GENERAL DIFFERENTIATION RESOURCES		
TITLE	**DESCRIPTION**	**AVAILABLE AT . . .**
Curriculum Compacting: The Complete Guide to Modifying the Regular Curriculum for High Ability Students by Sally Reis, Deborah Burns & Joseph Renzulli	Everything teachers need to understand, justify, and implement curriculum compacting for advanced learners.	www.creativelearningpress.com
Curriculum Starter Cards: Developing Differentiated Lessons for Gifted Students by Sandra Kaplan & Michael Cannon	A collection of cards with differentiated learning experiences that emphasizes depth and complexity and includes independent study, student products, and higher level thinking.	www.prufrock.com
Developing the Gifts and Talents of all Students in the Regular Classroom by Margaret Beecher	Innovative K-12 curriculum model designed to reach all students in heterogeneous classrooms. It combines the Enrichment Triad Model with differentiated strategies.	www.creativelearningpress.com
The Differentiated Classroom: Responding to the Needs of All Learners by Carol Tomlinson	Definition of the differentiated classroom and the guiding principles with instructional strategies that support differentiation.	www.ascd.org
A Different Place	A website with differentiated activities in all content areas.	www.adifferentplace.org/index.html
Fredrick County Public Schools	Curriculum and instruction resources for extension, enrichment, and advancement in many different subject areas.	www.fcpsteach.org/gt_renzulli/default.cfm

TITLE	DESCRIPTION	AVAILABLE AT
How to Differentiate Instruction in Mixed-Ability Classrooms (2nd Edition) by Carol Tomlinson	A practical guide to addressing the diverse needs of students in mixed-ability classrooms.	www.ascd.org
The Schoolwide Enrichment Model: A How-To-Guide for Educational Excellence by Joseph Renzulli & Sally Reis,	A collection of instruments, charts, checklists, taxonomies, assessment tools, forms, and planning guides designed to help educators organize, administer, maintain, and evaluate different the Schoolwide Enrichment Model.	www.creativelearningpress.com
Strategies for Differentiating Instruction: Best Practices for the Classroom by Julia Roberts & Tracy Inman	Offers practical differentiation strategies for teachers to use in the classroom, including many Think-Tac-Toe samples.	www.prufrock.com
Understanding by Design by Grant Wiggins & Jay McTighe,	With a book, workbook, video and blackline masters, provides a wonderful way to differentiate curriculum as several different outcomes can be planned with similar or overlapping learning tasks.	www.ascd.org

INTEREST AND LEARNING STYLE SURVEYS & INVENTORIES

Getting to Know You	Survey to gather information about students' learning profiles and interests in order to guide instructional planning and to differentiate accordingly.	www.fcpsteach.org
If I Ran the School	Survey designed to identify areas of interest among students, and thus possible teaching topics in the classroom.	www.gifted.uconn.edu/3summers/pdf/ifiran.pdf
Interest-a-Lyzer Family of Instruments	Six interest assessment tools that comprise the Interest-A-Lyzer "Family of Instruments."	www.creativelearningpress.com

Title	Description	Available At
Learning Style Inventory	Elementary and middle school inventories that help students and teachers hone in on preferred learning styles, such as independent study, direct instruction, technology, and discussion.	www.creativelearningpress.com
My Way . . . An Expression Style Instrument	An inventory to help students and teachers create a profile that reflects a student's preference for creating different types of products.	www.gifted.uconn.edu/sem/pdf/myway.pdf
Scholastic Interest Inventory	Interest inventory from Scholastic appropriate for upper elementary students.	teacher.scholastic.com/LessonPlans/unit_roadtosuccess_invent.pdf
Total Talent Portfolio	A method for compiling and analyzing each student's unique talent profile in order to choose the best enrichment and acceleration options.	www.creativelearningpress.com
What are YOU interested in?	Pictorial interest inventory for K-2 students.	www.fcpsteach.org
Who Are You? What Do You Like?	Interest inventory for students in grades 3-5.	www.fcpsteach.org

QUESTIONING RESOURCES

The Art of Questioning	Examples of low-inquiry and high-inquiry questions.	scied.gsu.edu/Hassard/mos/8.3c.html
Open-ended Assessment in Math	Examples of open-ended math problems for all levels.	books.heinemann.com/math/construct.cfm

TIERED ACTIVITIES

Differentiated Curriculum Samples	K–12 tiered activities from the state of Oregon.	www.openc.k12.or.us/reaching/tag/dcsamples.html

Title	Description	Available At
Tiered Curriculum Project	Tiered activities in math, language arts, and science for grades K–12.	ideanet.doe.state.in.us/ exceptional/gt/tiered_curriculum

PROBLEM-BASED LEARNING

Edutopia – Project Based Learning	Information on project-based service learning activities.	www.edutopia.org/ projectbasedlearning
Exploring the Environment: Teacher Pages	Excellent background information on PBL, plus sample modules for 5– 12 grades.	www.cotf.edu/ete/teacher/teacher-out.html
FermiLab's Science Adventures	PBL activities with a technology emphasis	ed.fnal.gov/index.shtml

INDEPENDENT OR SMALL GROUP INVESTIGATIONS

Chi Square, Pie-Charts and Me by Susan Baum, Bob Gable, & Karen List	Helps students differentiate between 'real world' research and report writing, clarify and elaborate on the diffcrent kinds of research and the specific steps necessary to conduct a research project.	www.rfwp.com
Independent Investigation Method by Cindy Nottage & Virginia Morse	A teacher-friendly research process, adaptable to your own curriculum and differentiated according to your students' grade level and achievement level.	www.iimresearch.com
Kids Guide to Social Action by Barbara A. Lewis	Shows kids how to write letters, conduct interviews, make speeches, take surveys, raise funds, get media coverage.	www.freespirit.com
Looking for Data in all the Right Places by Alana Starko & Gina Schack	Takes students out of the library and into the real world! Excellent guidebook to help students learn how to gather and analyze data to answer their research questions.	www.creativelearningpress.com

Title	Description	Available At
WebQuest.org	Contains over 2500 webquests and a search engine to find what you want!	webquest.org/search/index.php

SPECIFIC CONTENT AREA RESOURCES

Language Arts		
Center for Gifted Education Language Arts Curriculum Units	Units that develop students' skills in literary analysis and interpretation, persuasive writing, linguistic competency, and oral communication, as well as strengthen students' reasoning skills and understanding of the concept of change.	cfge.wm.edu/curr_language.htm
Cummings Study Guides	Study guides for the Great Works of World Literature including guides for all the plays and poems of William Shakespeare.	www.cummingsstudyguides.net
Junior Great Books	Literature program designed to develop essential literacy skills through shared inquiry discussions.	www.greatbooks.org
Michael Clay Thompson Language Arts Curriculum	Inspiring and engaging books full of language activities.	www.rfwp.com/mct.php
Some of My Best Friends Are Books by Judith Halsted	To aid in choosing appropriate reading materials, contains over 200 pages of annotated bibliographic references organized by grade level groupings with plot summaries and discussion ideas.	www.giftedbooks.com
Mathematics		
Figure This!	Math challenges that encourage problem solving.	www.figurethis.org

Title	Description	Available At
Mentoring Mathematical Minds	Challenging and motivational math units for grades 3–5 that concentrate on communication, reasoning, connections, and problem solving.	www.projectm3.org
National Council of Teachers of Mathematics: Illuminations	Resources that help improve the teaching and learning of mathematics for all students.	illuminations.nctm.org
The National Library of Virtual Manipulative for Interactive Mathematics	A library of uniquely interactive, web-based virtual manipulatives or concept tutorials for K–12 math instruction	nlvm.usu.edu/en/nav/index.html
NRICH	Free mathematics enrichment resources for pupils of all ages.	nrich.maths.org/public
RekenWeb	Support for primary school teachers in their task to teach realistic mathematics and challenge students with included online activities.	http://www.fi.uu.nl/rekenweb/en/
Science		
Center for Gifted Education Science Curriculum	Units challenge students to analyze real-world problems, understand the concept of systems, and design and conduct scientific experiments.	cfge.wm.cdu/curr_science.htm
Exploratorium	Extremely engaging science experiments on hundreds of different topics.	www.exploratorium.org/
HowStuffWorks	Shows kids how things like pyramids, transmissions, and the iPhone work.	www.howstuffworks.com
Rader's Kapili.com	Portal to introductory science sites on chemistry, biology, geography, physics, and the cosmos.	www.kapili.com
Solar System Exploration	Lesson plans about the Solar System, space travel, and everything related to it.	solarsystem.nasa.gov/educ/lessons.cfm

TITLE	DESCRIPTION	AVAILABLE AT
Social Studies		
Center for Gifted Education Social Studies Curriculum	Social studies units that emphasize primary source analysis, critical thinking, and concept development to help students develop understanding of high-level social studies content in key areas.	cfge.wm.edu/curr_socialstudies.htm
The Learning Page	Access to over 100 collections in the Library of Congress' American Memory Project	memory.loc.gov/learn/
National Geographic Kids	Many animal activities and a few geography ones too.	kids.nationalgeographic.com
Interdisciplinary		
Interact	Ready-to-use interdisciplinary simulations that encourage K–12 students to learn in a variety of ways.	www.highsmith.com/webapp/wcs/stores/servlet/Production/Search.jsp?catalogId=10050&storeId=10001&langId=-1&N=796
Smithsonian	A variety of interdisciplinary lessons for K-12.	http://smithsonianeducation.org/educators/lesson_plans/history_culture.html

GIFTED EDUCATION AND ADVOCACY RESOURCES

Resources for Teachers, Parents, and Students		
The Association for the Gifted	National advocacy group in support of professionals and parents work with gifted children.	www.cectag.org
Davidson Institute for Talent Development	Links to information for and about gifted students, their parents and educators, including Young Scholars and Fellows programs.	www.ditd.org

TITLE	DESCRIPTION	AVAILABLE AT
Gifted Education Resource Institute (GERI) at Purdue University	Gifted education center that provides challenging PreK-12 Saturday and summer enrichment programs, conducts research, and offers graduate programs.	www.purdue.edu/geri
Guiding the Gifted Child: A Practical Source for Parents and *Teachers* by James Webb	Excellent book with a focus on social and emotional issues that gifted children encounter.	www.giftedbooks.com
Hoagies' Gifted Education Page	A comprehensive gifted website with links to full text articles on a wide variety of topics.	www.hoagiesgifted.org
National Association for Gifted Children	National advocacy group in support of gifted youth and their education.	www.nagc.org
National Research Center on the Gifted and Talented	National research center that disseminates information on "best practices" in gifted education.	www.gifted.uconn.edu/nrcgt
Supporting Emotional Needs of the Gifted (SENG)	Advocacy group with a focus on social and emotional needs of gifted individuals.	www.sengifted.org
Resources for Teachers		
Enrichment Clusters: A Practical Plan for Real-World, Student-Driven Learning by Joseph Renzulli, Marcia Gentry, & Sally Reis	Step-by-step guide on how to set up a student-driven Enrichment Cluster Program with exciting opportunities for students to delve into areas of strong interest.	www.creativelearningpress.com
Teaching with Love and Logic: Taking Control of the Classroom by Jim Fay and David Funk	Positive approach to teaching and classroom management that fosters student independence and responsibility.	www.loveandlogic.com
Teaching Young Gifted Children in the Regular Classroom: Identifying, Nurturing, and Challenging Ages 4-9 by Joan Smutny, Sally Walker, & Elizabeth Meckstroth	Practical, easy to read guide for teachers.	www.freespirit.com

TITLE	DESCRIPTION	AVAILABLE AT
Resources for Parents		
Genius Denied: How to Stop Wasting Our Brightest Minds by Jan and Bob Davidson	Practical advice from founders of a nonprofit organization that assists gifted children.	www.geniusdenied.com
Helping Gifted Children Soar: A Practical Guide for Parents and Teachers by Carol Strip	An readable, user-friendly guide-book for parents and teachers.	www.giftedbooks.com
Mellow Out, They Say. If I Only Could: Intensities and Sensitivities of the Young and Bright by Michael M. Piechowski	An examination of the emotional sensitivities and intensities of gifted youth.	www.mellowout.us/order.html
Nation Deceived by Nicholas Colangelo, Susan Assouline, & Miraca Gross	National report on the practice of acceleration.	www.nationdeceived.org
The Optimistic Child: A Proven Program to Safeguard Children Against Depression and Build-Lifelong Resilience by Martin Seligman	A positive approach to parenting that teaches children the skill of optimism to combat pessimism and its disastrous consequences: depressed mood, resignation, underachievement, and even un-expectedly poor physical health.	Book available at www.amazon.com; additional information on Positive Psychology at www.authentichappiness.sas.upenn.edu
Parenting with Love and Logic by Foster Cline and Jim Fay	Strategies that encourage children to develop problem solving skills while minimizing friction and power struggles between parents and children.	www.loveandlogic.com
Raising your Spirited Child Revised Edition: A Guide for Parents whose Child is more Intense, Sensitive, Perceptive, Persistent, Energetic by Mary Sheedy Kurcinka.	Guide to help parents of high intensity children. Provides strategies, support systems, and information to help parent such children successfully.	www.harpercollins.com/books/9780060739669/Raising_Your_Spirited_Child_Rev_Ed/index.aspx
The Social and Emotional Development of Gifted Children: What Do We Know? Edited by: Maureen Neihart, Sally Reis, Nancy Robinson, Sidney Moon	Comprehensive guide to the social and emotional lives of gifted children and youth covering issues related to underachieve-ment, sensitivity, depression, and loneliness.	www.prufrock.com

TITLE	DESCRIPTION	AVAILABLE AT

PUBLISHERS OF MATERIALS RELATED TO GIFTEDNESS

TITLE	DESCRIPTION	AVAILABLE AT
Creative Learning Press	A wide variety of program manuals for gifted education teachers and activity or how-to books for students.	www.creativelearningpress.com
Creative Publications	High level teaching resources in all content areas.	www.creativepublications.com/
Critical Thinking Co.	Great critical thinking resources for teachers and parents.	www.criticalthinking.com
Dale Seymour Publications	Student activity books focused on problem solving.	plgcatalog.pearson.com
Free Spirit Press	Books that focus on learning tools that support young people's social and emotional health.	www.freespirit.com
Great Potential Press	Books and videos for parents and teachers of gifted children.	www.giftedbooks.com/
National Association for Gifted Children	Books and journals including Gifted Child Quarterly, Parenting for High Potential, and Teaching for High Potential.	www.nagc.org
Prufrock Press	Extensive collection of products focused on gifted education, gifted children, and advanced academic education. Publishes journal Gifted Child Today.	www.prufrock.com

PROGRAMS FOR GIFTED, CREATIVE, AND TALENTED STUDENTS

TITLE	DESCRIPTION	AVAILABLE AT
Center for Innovative and Talented Youth, University of Denver	Conducts Rocky Mountain talent search for highly-able youth in grades 3-9 and offers summer and academic year programs for students in grades K-12.	www.du.edu/city

Title	Description	Available At
Center for Talent Development, Northwestern University	Conducts Midwest talent search for highly-able youth, provides challenging online courses for students in grades K–12, and offers summer and academic year programs for students in grades PreK–12.	www.ctd.northwestern.edu
Continental Mathematics League	Mathematics problem solving competition for students in grades 2-12.	www.continentalmathematic-sleague.com/
Destination Imagination	Focuses on the process, art, and skill associated with problem solving.	www.destinationimagination.org
Duke University Talent Identification Program	Conducts talent search in the southeast region for highly-able youth in grades 4-7, provides challenging online courses for students in grades 8–12, and offers summer programs for students in grades 7-12.	www.tip.duke.edu
The Education Program for Gifted Youth (EPGY) at Stanford University	Computer-based distance-learning courses for high-ability students of all ages addressing a variety of subjects at levels ranging from kindergarten through advanced-undergraduate.	http://epgy.stanford.edu/
Future Problem Solving Program International	Creative problem-solving program that stimulates critical and creative thinking skills and encourages students to develop a vision for the future.	www.fpsp.org
Invention Convention	Invention program that gives students an opportunity to think creatively, experiment, and work with data as they invent a new product or process.	www.eduplace.com/science/in-vention/overview.html
Johns Hopkins University: Center for Talented Youth	Conducts talent search for highly able youth in grades 2–8, provides challenging online courses for students in grades K–12, and offers summer programs for students in grades 2–12.	www.cty.jhu.edu

TITLE	DESCRIPTION	AVAILABLE AT
Math Olympiads	Contains mathematics contests for elementary and middle school groups.	www.moems.org
Odyssey of the Mind	A creative problem-solving program for K-12 students that challenges them to apply their creativity to solve problems ranging from building mechanical devices to presenting interpretations of literary classics.	www.odysseyofthemind.org
Science Olympiad	Presents elementary and secondary Science Olympiad tournaments with an emphasis on teamwork, problem-solving and hand-on, minds-on constructivist learning practices.	www.soinc.org
University of Iowa, College of Education Belin-Blank Center	Conducts talent search for highly-able youth in grades 2-9, and offers summer and academic year programs for students in grades 2-12.	www.education.uiowa.edu/belin-blank/talent-search/howtoreg.asp

Marcia Gentry, Ph. D.

Marcia Gentry serves as Director of the Gifted Education Resource Institute at Purdue University where she is associate professor of educational studies and where she directs the doctoral program in gifted education. She very much enjoys her work with her doctoral students. Her research has focused on the use of cluster grouping and differentiation; the application of gifted education pedagogy to improve teaching and learning; student perceptions of school; and on non-traditional services and underserved populations—areas in which she has over 50 publications. Dr. Gentry developed and studied the Total School Cluster Grouping Model and is engaged in continued research on its effects concerning student achievement and identification and on teacher practices. She is active in the National Association of Gifted Children and in the American Educational Research Association, and she serves on the editorial boards of the major journals in the field of gifted education. She completed her Ph.D. at the University of Connecticut in 1996. Prior to her graduate work, she was both a teacher and a gifted education coordinator in Michigan. She also conducts professional development workshops on a variety of topics related to gifted education and improving schools using talent development. Marcia also enjoys learning about schools through the eyes of her daughter, who is currently in elementary school.

Rebecca L. Mann, Ph.D.

Becky Mann is the Co-Director of the Gifted Education Resource Institute and an Assistant Professor of Educational Studies at Purdue University where she oversees the PreKindergarten through 12th grade talent development programs and the gifted and talented licensure program. Her areas of research and interest include visual spatial learners, twice exceptional students, and differentiating the curriculum. She has conducted workshops in school districts throughout 15 states on the characteristics of gifted learners and how to differentiate the curriculum to meet their academic needs. In addition, Becky presents regularly at state and national conferences including the National Association for Gifted Children, Confratute, and the DISCOVER! Institute. She completed her Ph.D. at the University of Connecticut in 2005. Prior to her doctoral studies she was a gifted and talented coordinator and resource teacher and an elementary classroom teacher in Colorado and New Hampshire, where she was named the 2001 Educator of the Year of the Gifted.